Retire Early with Passive Income

Retire Early with Passive Income
The Millennial's guide to Passive Income Savings

By Kevin Kunkle

**Copyright © 2019 by Kevin Kunkle and Step Next Training LLC. And Step Next Publishing
Version 1.0**

**All Rights Reserved
First Printing, 2019**

Visit Our Website at: www.stepnexttraining.com

Table of Contents

Introduction
Why Everyone is Not a Millionaire
- 1) Intro
- 2) The Problem
- 3) The Reward

Know Your Stuff
- 4) Definition of Terms
- 5) Types of Expenses
- 6) Passive Income vs. Active Income
- 7) Level out the Peaks and Valleys
- 8) Variable Income Converted to Steady Passive Income

How Anyone Can be a Millionaire
- 9) The Easiest Way to Make 1 Million Dollars
- 10) The Foundation that You Will Build Up From
- 11) Creating a Passive Income Account
- 12) How to Find a 10% CAGR Fund
- 13) Inflation and Harder Math

Real Life Examples
- 14) Relatable Characters
- 15) Set your Goal
- 16) Pay your Cable Bill with Passive Income
- 17) Never worry About Your Mortgage Payment Again
- 18) Pay Your Monthly Bills with Passive Income
- 18) Never Pay a Car Payment Ever Again
- 19) How Much do You Need to Retire?
- 20) Retire Early

Acknowledgments

I have to start by thanking my farther, Bernard. He taught me to look at the bigger picture of life, to set goals and build a plan to achieve them. And thank you for being the editor for this book.

I would like to thank my wife and kids for being so supportive during the months it took to write this book, and for the endless times I said: "I think I have 2 more pages over and over again.

Intro

Why are you reading this book? You want out of the Grind. You want to get out of the rat race. You want to be financially independent. You want to make your money work for you.

The number 1 thing that people worry about is paying their Bills; number 2 is not having enough Money. So let's change that and create a life where you do not need to worry about Bills or Money. Let's allow your money to create more money, at a rate that pays your bills and removes that stress from your life. Look at this article from Psychologicalhealthcare.com
https://www.psychologicalhealthcare.com.au/blog/youre-not-alone-top-things-people-worry-most-about/

60% - 70% of Americans have $0-$1,000 in their savings. They have no incentive to save. And yet, the median household income is ~$60,000 in the year 2018. This means that there is a lack of interest in savings in the United States even though there is enough money in most households. There have been many other countries that have had this problem and at a worse rate than the US. And one proven solution is a lottery-linked savings account. Many states in the US are experimenting with it now, as well as a Prize-Linked Savings (PLS). What these do is create excitement in saving more money by tapping into the fun and excitement of the lottery system. By entering money into these accounts, you are entered into quarterly lotteries that could pay out hundreds of thousands of dollars. If you want to find out more about this concept, please visit Freakonomics article. http://freakonomics.com/podcast/freakonomics-radio-could-a-lottery-be-the-answer-to-americas-poor-savings-rate/

This book aims to create that same excitement, by showing the power of passive income. This book is about Setting Goals that are not just about "Building Wealth". This book will allow you to create accounts that will pay for your cable bill; an account that pays for your mortgage payment each year; and an account that allows you to retire at any age. These are goals that seem out of reach for most people, but that is just not true. Some people think that in order to retire they need to win the lottery which again is not true. If you want to achieve the feeling of winning the lottery with just using your own money to create an environment that feels like winning the lottery. I have made the math in the book very easy to follow and made the steps to follow also very easy. If you passed high school math, you can follow this book well enough to show you the road map to setting and achieving these goals. This book will walk you through step by step how to create the account and build it up to be able to retire. If you do not think you can afford this, I will say this: "Save $4 dollars a day." That is all you need to get started. With $4 a day, you create an account paying 11.5% a year and create $1,000,000 in just forty years of time. That is enough to retire without considering Social Security, 401K, Roth IRA, or other savings accounts. $4 is all you need. That is the power of time. The more time you have, the easier it gets. But if you have less time and you want to retire when you are 42 years old, all you need to do is save $1,000 a month (20% of the median household income). At $1,000 a month, you can achieve a $1,000,000 in just 22 years. We are not just talking about the 1% of income families, we are talking about every income family. We are not talking about double downing your savings inputs to 40% of your monthly income. This book uses examples of people making $50,000 all the way to $200,000 and more. If you live in that range, follow this book and you find the particular path that represents you the best.

    You are reading this book because you want to achieve financial Independence and start living your life the way you want to. This book will teach you how to achieve the goals that you set, help you separate from the daily grind, and start enjoying the freedom that financial independence offers you. Imagine the bank sending you a check each month large enough for all of your utility bills, your mortgage payment, and even your car payments. What would you do if it existed? Would you sell everything in your house and travel the world? Would you Fire your Boss, and tell them where to stick their job? Would you go back to school and redefine yourself with the career that you always wanted to do instead of your current job? Would you start a creative venture like Painting or Writing a book? Or maybe you would keep the job, but just reduce your anxiety levels about paying the bills each and every month.

A little about the author to understand the viewpoint of the author. I grew up in the 80s and 90s. I had parents that are baby boomers. Like most Gen X/Y I was taught the value of hard work, and heard this quote weekly: "Work Hard, Get good grades, be Loyal and you will do well in life." You might be fortunate to retire early at the age of 55 from the same company that you worked for the whole time. I did great in school, even skipped my senior year of high school and went to college early. I was that guy. I landed a job at one of the biggest companies in the world. I worked hard. I traveled for work and lived out of a suitcase and was home for 11 days in total my first year working. Working hard was an understatement. I saved 98% of my salary for my first years building up a large nest egg. I kept the hard-working attitude throughout the next 15 years. I was following the GenX playbook and had my nose to the grindstone. I was highly rewarded and compensated for my efforts. I looked at Millennials and said they are lazy and want more than they deserve. And what I found out was my loyalty and hard work went out the window and I was caught in an upper management fight throughout my organization. So having to redefine myself, I found out that I was doing it wrong. I learned that hard work and loyalty was not the equation that worked in the current culture anymore. The Millennials demanding more and jumping from company to company is the new norm. Having side hustles and following passions is the new way of doing things. Gaps between jobs are growing and are more common than not. The average years spent with a company for younger people are 3.2 years and declining. When I found this, I was shocked, horrified, and stressed. I had to ask myself "Was I doing it wrong".

After 20 years of working for one of the largest companies in a high paying very secure job, I found this large company went through hard times and eliminated my sector. Not because of my performance, not because of my 20 years of heavily awarded service, not because it was the correct or incorrect decision, but purely because I was in the wrong place at the wrong time for the company. I grew up in the 80/90s and we were always told that if you work hard and be loyal that you would be rewarded with a steady job and high wages. Well, this was true for the 1990s and 2000s. But I learned this important lesson. "No job is bulletproof". I used my nest egg to span the gap and redefine myself. I am an Engineer by schooling, but spent 17 years building skills as a Problem-Solving Expert creating process after process that saved the company millions each year. I spent the last 17 years working for this company asking this simple question every day: "There has to be a better way to do this" and than creating process after process that saved the company millions each year. So after I exited this company, I woke up every day saying the same mantra. "There has to be a better way to do this".

Passive incomes were where I pointed to first. Using the money that I had in savings accounts to start making more money, and using those investments to pay the bills. My objectives changed. I went from trying to get a new job that would get me the best salary to "how can I make my money make more money". I studied ultra Rich people and asked how did they do it. Removing the ones that created the next big computer app/game/utility, I found a pattern. Here is the real secret of Big Money. <u>Work to Invest, not to Spend.</u> Live off your investments not your salary. Create accounts that use the money to make more money than the rate that you spend. Look at two famous American Millionaires. Richer than Bill Gates and Warren Buffet were John D. Rockefeller and Cornelius Vanderbilt. They were both rags to riches stories and died with hundreds of Billions in today's dollars. But what is most interesting about these families is how the money was spent by their children. Rockefeller instilled the value of saving to his children and grandchildren and now the great-grandchildren still have a large part of the family fortune. Where the Vanderbilt Family is the opposite story, the family has spent the money like they needed to become bankrupt. So follow the Rockefeller family and create investments that pay year after year. The method is correct whether you are starting with $300 Billion dollars or just $300 dollars.

This research again changed the way I looked at life. I started to ask the question "What would it take to have enough in investment for me to retire" and never have to work again. I dove into spreadsheets to find the answer. This book was created from the notes I took for my own personal case study. Your results will vary from mine, but I will give you the strategy and details needed to do the Math needed to fund your financial goals. The math is not hard, and I will walk you through it easily enough for you to follow along with your exact numbers.

The steps are easy: Set a Financial Goal, Find the length of time needed to complete your goal, Create a "Passive Income" Account, Invest per your Financial Plan. After that, sit back and enjoy the checks coming in each and every month. Creating that financial security that you have been looking for.

If you are sitting there and are in massive credit card debt and your monthly income is less than your expenses, well you need to put this book down and get your house in order before you can walk this path to Millions. I refer you to Dave Ramsey Baby book ***The Total Money Makeover*** and get your Emergency Account, and debt paid off. Then come back to this book when you have the ability to start saving and creating your passive income account.

The Disclaimer
Kevin Kunkle is NOT an attorney, accountant, tax advisor, financial advisor, investment advisor, trader, dealer, broker, nor am I holding myself out to be. All investment/financial opinions expressed in this book are from personal research and experience of the author and are intended as educational material. This is not legal advice nor should you treat it as a substitute for legal

counsel or the services of a certified financial advisor. This book has been prepared for information purposes only and is not intended to provide and should not be relied on for, tax, legal or accounting advice. You should consult your own tax, legal and accounting advisors. I cannot be held responsible for any errors or omissions, and I accept no liability whatsoever for any loss or damage you may incur. The performance of investments listed in this book are historical data and past performance is not a reliable indicator of future results and investors may not see similar returns. The value of investment greatly fluctuates. Do your own Research and use multiple locations to congregate your own opinion, you should not rely solely on any one source of information to make any investment decision.

The Problem

<u>Everyone wants to get something for nothing</u>. Well, you can. Here is a little secret. All of those 1%ers know something that everyone else does not know. You might have heard the quote: **"Rich people don't work for money, money works for them"?** What does this mean? The secret is: they invest all of the money they collect from their jobs and live off the interest from their investments. They grow their wealth and only pull a portion of the interest each year to live on. A rich person with a $1,000,000 account which makes 10% in investments each year will live off of that $100,000 for the

year. Their salary is not touched; it goes into the account to build their wealth. So if they make $200,000 they will invest it into the wealth account and at the turn of the year, they will have $1.2 Million in the bank and then take out $120,000 next year to live. Unlike new rich music performers buying multiple Ferraris each year so they have interesting Instagram posts and go bankrupt 5 years after their last album. True rich people do not spend that money on crazy cars, they invest their money guaranteeing that they will never go bankrupt. They will never worry about paying for rent, never worry about paying the gas bill, not worrying if the refrigerator stops working or walking into a restaurant and not worrying if they buy the largest steak on the menu. Allowing them to live life to the fullest. Living a life that they create. Having time and money to do what they want to do. Money doesn't buy happiness but it can remove worries and concerns from your daily lives.

How does that sound to you? How does it sound if you had $100,000 delivered on your doorstep year after year after year? Would it seem like you hit the lottery? Would it seem too good to be true? Well if you follow the teaching of this book, I will show you how to go from $0 in the bank to live off your interest. This method is not just for the rich, it is for everyone. If you make the average US household income, you have more than enough to become a millionaire. The only question is how fast can it happen for you. The more you invest, the faster you will get there. If you already have $1 Million in the bank, it is easy for you to invest 100% of your job's salary into an investment account. Well, what about just 2% of the US average salary, can you handle not spending just 2% of your salary? If you can invest $120 a month wisely you will become a millionaire. This book will teach you how to convert $120 a month into 1 million dollars. If you can increase that amount to $200 or more it will take you shorter in time.

<u>Job stability</u> is something that people have craved generation after generation. Now Job Stability is something that is far and few between. Companies and the active income industry are transitioning to a place where Freelance work becomes more the norm than ever before.

The average time you spend with each company is decreasing rapidly. One reason is that businesses pop up fast and go away faster than ever before. Large companies get into trouble and sell off part of the company. So People are losing their active income, over circumstances out of their control for many reasons

1) The market for the business dries up or shifts. Look at General Electric. The Gas Power Plant Market has dried up which caused a ripple effect by removing (2) CEOs and countless lower level jobs all because the Market dried up.
2) Job descriptions are changing. If you went to school as an architect in the 90s (when Computers were barely a thing in college) and you focused on structural analysis on paper, you could be

replaced. Now, most structural analysis is being done by Computer inputs. If you were the guy that sat in the corner and crunched the numbers you might have been replaced by current technology or soon to be replaced by future A.I. technologies. You will be able to find work by pivoting into a similar job, or maybe do freelance work, but that old job title might not be a thing anymore.
3) Your health takes you out of your current job. Things happen and you might get sick, ill, disabled, and you find yourself not capable of doing the current job. That just means that you need to redefine your skill sets and adapt to the disability and pivot around it.

In 1960 the average lifespan of a company was 60 years and staying with a company your entire career was common. As of 2010, the average lifespan of a company was 15 years. Staying with one company your entire career will be almost impossible.

The overall statement is that active income streams are becoming unstable in the 21st century. The Gaps between active income streams will become larger and more frequent over time. So the question becomes this. Are you diversifying your revenue streams or are you relying on just one stream of income? A Diversified Income means that you are creating income in multiple ways. An example is this. Jen works as a Retail Manager and earns $50,000 a year. She also has a Youtube Knitting channel, making $1,000 a year. She also has a blog that pulls in $300 a year. Those side hustles are not making much income now because Jen is not devoting a lot of time against them, but during harder times she can raise those platforms up and achieve more revenue that way. These side income streams are getting easier and easier to start every day. If you have a conversation with a 20-year-old, they all know this and they are already capitalizing on it. Mechanical engineering students in college are running a side business of creating 3D printed objects for clients out of their room to pay for their daily pizza fix.

There are two types of people, the ones that do not save and the ones that save too much.
67% -71% of Americans have less than $5,000 in their savings account depending on which article you read on this topic. That means if you are in a group of 10 people, then 7 of you are not saving enough. Not having $5,000 in the bank for a rainy day can create a debt spiral and create financial ruin. For this group, they need to get a handle on their expenses and create an extra money gap between salary and expenses.

On the flip side, 20% of retirees in America have over $1,000,000 in savings and collecting social security and maybe pension as well. For many years financial planners have been advertising that people need a goal of $1,000,000+ to retire well and these 20% believed them without doing the math themselves. This side of the pendulum is much, much, much better than the other side, but this group also spent more years working hard at a job then they might have needed to. Most of this group will pass away with a large lump sum passed to their children, which is an honorable and exceptional gift to their children. If that was the intent of saving that much then they can pass away knowing that they have accomplished the goal of giving financial security to their children.

So why are people not investing in their future? https://www.fool.com/retirement/2018/03/15/5-reasons-americans-arent-saving-for-retirement-to.aspx

Motley fool has a list of stated reasons why no one invests in retirement. They state that either financial issues, blame debt, or their company is to blame. I do not believe what they are saying. I think it is this. It is not Sexy. There is no instant gratification when it comes to investing. They do not see the connection between investing and becoming a Millionaire. If I told someone tomorrow that if you give me $100 this month I will give you $10,000 in 40 years, I believe the answer will be No. If the answer was $100,000 (10 Times the interest Rate compounding, I bet the answer would still be no. So what if the problem.

It is not sexy enough.

So let's make investing Sexy. Let's talk about Free stuff, Let's talk about Firing your boss, Let's talk about retiring at the age of 33. Let's talk about retiring and traveling the world. Let's talk about leasing a supercar. Let's talk about Free Money through true passive income.

Let's talk about an account that pays your cable bill
Let's talk about an account that buys you a new car every 7 years
Let's talk about an account that pays your rent.
Let's talk about an account that allows you to retire at any age.
Let's talk about becoming so financial free that you do not worry about your bills anymore and you are working for fun following a passion
Let's talk about firing your boss and traveling the world while you can still enjoy it.

These are the Sexy thoughts that everyone wants and this is not hard to do. It takes going to an online bank and setting up an online brokerage account. I timed myself and it literally took 20 mins to set up. So take a Tuesday night and signup. I have no affiliation with any bank so choose yours based on a little research. Kiplinger's is that Magazine your dad used to read. But they have great lists of best brokerage accounts https://www.kiplinger.com/article/investing/T023-C000-S002-the-best-online-brokers-2018.html. Each has their own pros and cons, so match up with your best fit, or must pick the top on the list. Either way just choose to invest.

The reward

Imagine a world where you do not need to work and still be emotional well. Imagine a level of financial security that allows your normal "needed" expenses to be taken care for. Imagine getting a free direct deposit into your checking account large enough to pay all of your regular bills, creating an emotional well being around your own personal finances. This can create the ability to take that trip you always wanted to go on, going back for the college class that you wish you had time to attend, having the ability to take your wife on a getaway that you could never afford.

No amount of money can buy you happiness or love, but it can remove worries and concerns about how you are going to eat today, where you are going to live, and how you will afford your health care when you are older. Once you have enough money that those worries are eliminated, you will have the luxury of time to find happiness, love, and fulfillment. A study by Purdue University and the University of Virginia Psychologists have stated that emotional well-being needs between $65k-$75K.

When you remove the need for an active income the options are endless. You can remove the need for your current job, which can allow you to retire and relax., Or you can go back to school and start another career, or even stay in your current position save more, so you can buy a sports car that you always wanted. Time will be finally on your side, and allow you to choose paths of happiness instead of doing the "Right" thing.

Retiring early. How does it sound to retire at 45, 40 or even 35? Well, you can do that. All it takes is discipline and some simple math. Everything is possible. If you are a software designer and want to quit your job and become a beach bum and teach kids how to water ski, I will show you how. It takes money, time and discipline to achieve a goal like that, but it is not unheard of. In this book, we will show you how to use your money to create more money. Imagine retiring in at the age of 30 to hike around the world. Imagine firing your boss to start your career as an Architect. Imagine a time when you are not worried about paying the electric bill. Imagine a time when money just magically shows up in your account when you were not even trying.

If you save enough you can have money flowing freely into your checking account large enough to allow you buy all the things on your Amazon wish list, or remodel your house room by room or even a new car.

Definition of Terms

<u>Financial Independent</u>: Per the definition, on Dictionary.com @2018 the term <u>Independent</u> means "not influenced or controlled by others in matters of opinion, conduct, etc.; thinking or acting for oneself." The term Financial Independent means that your personal financial environment is not in the control or others and your financial environment is dependent on you and only you. When you do not need a job to live your financial life and pay your bills than you reach a financial environment that is Financial Independent.

<u>Financially Secure</u>: Per the definition, on Dictionary.com @2018 the term <u>Secure</u> means "free from or not exposed to danger or harm; safe." The term Financial Secure means that your personal financial environment is Safe. To be financially secure you need to feel safe about your financial environment. You need to know that your bills will be paid, there will be food on the table and you will have gas in your car. The amount that you need to have in order to financially secure between person to person.

Retire Early with Passive Income

59 and ½. "Golden Age" This is the official Age in which you can start pulling from your 401k without any penalties. Before the age of 59 and ½, you will need to pay a penalty of 10%. There are exceptions to the rule and there are some possibilities that you can start to pull from the account at the age of 55. But in the effort of keeping things simple, we will use the Age of "60" as a rounded 59 and ½.

Interest: Per the definition on Yourdictionary.com @2018 the term Interest means "An amount of money that an investor receives for leaving funds on deposit in an interest-bearing account, usually expressed in annual percentage terms." If your bank savings account has a 2% interest rate and you give the bank $100 than in a year the bank will pay you $2 dollars for keeping your money for a full year. This makes your $100 worth $102 at the end of the first year.

Inflation: Per the definition, on Yourdictionary.com @2018 the term Inflation means "Inflation is defined as an increase in the amount of money and credit in the economy in relation to the supply of goods and services." The more money that exists means the value of each dollar goes down. If you were able to buy a candy bar in the year 2000 for $1 and the US government creates more money into the economy by printing more dollars. Well, the $1 Dollar that we had in 2000 is now worth less than in 2018. This means that the candy bar is not worth $1 dollar so the candy company raises its price by the inflation amount of 3% per year and is now worth $1.70 in 2018 dollars.

<u>AAGR: (Average Annualized Growth Rate):</u> When looking up the annual return rate most websites and magazines use AAGR and state the annual return. It is simple to calculate. You look at the past five years returns and average them. Any simple excel program can do this calculation but there is so many websites that offers this information that you can just go to morningstar.com and find the information you are looking for. An example of the calculation is Apple stock during the years from 2000 to 2004

Year	Annual Return
2000	-71%
2001	47%
2002	-34%
2003	49%
2004	201%

The average on investment is
(-71+47-34+49+201)/5 = 38%.
Using AAGR you could predict that a $1,000 investment would grow $380 each year compounded.

Year	Annual Return	Investment
2000	38%	$1,380
2001	38%	$1,904
2002	38%	$2,628
2003	38%	$3,627
2004	38%	$5,005

If you were receiving 38% each year your return on $1,000 would be $5,000.

CAGR: (Compound Annual Growth Rate): There is an error with using AAGR to calculate what your actual growth is. The CAGR is the actual growth of your investment over that same time period. With CAGR you use an investment amount and you multiply your investment by the return of each year's actual return. The best way to show the difference between AAGR and CAGR is to show the math.

Year	Annual Return	Investment
2000	-71%	$290
2001	47%	$426
2002	-34%	$281
2003	49%	$419
2004	201%	$1,262

So if you invested $1,000 in Apple stock on Jan 01 2000 the return on Dec 31, 2004, will be actually $1,262. It is not the $5,005 that the AAGR showed through its calculations. The reason for the difference is that negative years impact your investment more severe than it does the average. That first year demolishes the investment amount and drops your $1,000 investment all the way down to $290, so even in 2004 when the stock grew 201% it just barely breaks a profit from the original $1,000 investment. CAGR is a more accurate return estimate of what your actual return will be, it is just harder to calculate.

Retire Early with Passive Income

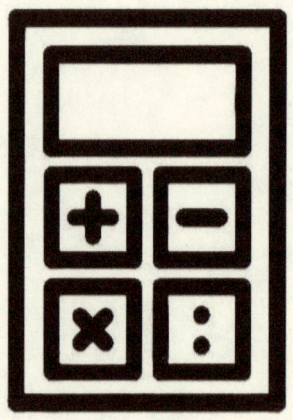

Types of Expenses

There are 4 types of expenses that are needed to create your budget.

Fixed Expenses are expenses that are the same month after month. Mortgage and cable bills are fixed expenses and can be planned for and easily budgeted.

A variable Expense is an expense that changes month to month. Your Electric, Gas, and Water bills are expenses that will vary month after month. These are harder to plan than fixed expenses but are predictable after a year of tracked charges.

Intermediate Expenses are expenses that are billed on a yearly or semi-yearly basis. So your insurance bills and house taxes are types of intermediate expenses that need to be paid once a year.

Discretionary Expenses are expenses that are not "needed". Bills like eating out, vacation, and entertainment items are expenses that can be eliminated if you lose your job or run into hard times.

There is one more item to look at when you are living on a budget. Your Expenses will increase over time. All bills except your mortgage will increase at a rate similar to the inflation rate of 3% a year after year. Hopefully, our active income increases at the same rate if not more than that over time.

If you run into hard times you need to eliminate your discretionary expenses and then look at your other expenses to reduce as much as you can. If you reduce the kids club activities, reduce the cable bill, and any eating out bills you could reduce their expenses from by $800 a month, making it easier to span between active income jobs. You might think to reduce the house payment by selling your house and getting the house equity but then you would lose 6% in expenses to sell the house. You could call and eliminate trash pickup and take the trash to the dump yourself, but let's face it you probably will not do that.

Those four expenses are needed to calculate your yearly expenses. Another type of expenses that needs to be watched is Transaction Expenses and Expense Ratio. These expenses are only needed when you are calculating an investment yearly return. All investments have expenses and either you pay for the fee to buy and sell stocks, mutual funds or other investments, this is called Transaction Expenses. Or you pay yearly a certain fee to be part of the investment which is called an Expense Ratio. When looking at investments you need to understand the fees and expenses with each expense. If you have a mutual fund that is returning 12% each year but has an expense ratio of 2%, your money will only grow at a rate of 10%. When deciding which investments are correct for you, you need to subtract any fees or expenses against the yearly return rate to plan accurately. In this book I will teach you how to set up a Passive Income account and show you how to use the interest each year to pay for your monthly bills, you can pull out the money every month or once a year. The less you buy and sell, the fewer fees you will pay. You want to reduce the number of fees as much as possible. If you are invested into stock and you want to sell some of that stock to pay for your monthly bills, you need to watch out for the sales fee. On average, most online brokerage sites have a stock trade fee of $5.00 when buying and selling your stocks. If you are selling stocks in the amount of $1000 to pay for your mortgage each month that $5 dollar fee will be 0.5% of the $1000. This means that you need to make 0.5% more each year just to pay for your fees. If you take out the money each quarter (every 3 months,) the amount of $3,000 to pay for the next 3 months of mortgage, then your trade fee is still $5 and the percentage is now reduced to 0.16%, so it is better to take out larger chunks of money. However, what is the interest that you are missing out if you take out 3 months of mortgage payments before you need it? If you are averaging 10% of return each year on your passive income account, then you make $100 each year on every $1000 you have invested. So on average, you will make $8.33 per month per $1000. So if you were to keep the money in your account as long as possible, you will earn $8 for every month you can keep it in the account. So the bottom line is that if you are taking out $1000 or more each month to pay for your bills, than you should sell stocks each month. But personally, I think that is too much work, so, I sell on the 1st of each quarter (Jan1st, April 1st, July 1st, and Oct 1st). Selling each month is too much work for me to make a profit of $3.00 each month, so selling each quarter is the right mix for me.

Passive Income vs. Active Income.

If you are reading this book you might have heard the term "Passive Income". There are many different definitions of the Term and even more get rich schemes promoting Passive Income. The definition I use is this: A "True passive" income is something that takes time to set up but then goes to zero amount of yearly effort/management in order to collect an income. The way to test a truly passive income is this. Do not touch, modify, advertise or even monitor a passive income for a full year and still collect a paycheck from it. Even if that account/job took you 20 to 200 hours to set up, that passive income stream is still passive if you do not need to manage it.

The opposite of passive income is "active Income", and it means an income that you received for your actions. So working for a company for 40 hours a week is considered Active Income. Active Income is a Temporary guarantee that you have a steady Income, which most people thrive for. It is an honorable and reliable way to make high wages for your efforts. Active Income is needed in order to establish your other streams of income. The higher the active income, the faster you can create your passive income. If you are a rich trust fund kid, you can skip the active income step of your life. But if you are not, get yourself a good job and collect an active income that will fund your passive income adventures.

There are many different ways to create passive income, some are more passive than others. Writing a Book can take up to 2 years or more. But once you finished the book, you can create income from the sales of the book. This can be considered Passive Income, but know that the first year of selling the book can be more active than passive. From publishing, advertising, and promoting through book signings and more, it can take up many hours a month to progress through that first year. Take John Green as an example, one of the largest authors of the 2000s. He is collecting money from the books that he has written but he is also doing a daily blog, working on movies and posts actively on social media. This is all part of his brand building to allow him to sell more books and other items associated with his brands. He could live in a cabin in the woods and still make millions, but being active and building a community allows him to enjoy life and grow his audience larger.

If you are an actor and collect active income from a TV show, that salary would be considered Active Income., But if that show is syndicated, then those royalty checks would be considered Passive Income since you do not have to do anything each year to collect royalties from the work that you complete years before.

      Some Real Estate Incomes can be considered as Passive income. If you Rent out houses to customers, there is not a lot of weekly effort needed to be able to receive the rent. But I would refer to the definition above because you can easily turn real estate into an active income. But if you hire a management firm to manage the repairs and maintenance on the house and hire an accountant to help with taxes, your yearly effort will be very small. The more passive you are, the less you will make on that investment. But it could still be considered passive. There are so many other Active and Passive income paths that I will not list them all.

      The Passive income that this book talks about is "Using Money to make money". Or "Make money work for you, instead of working for your money". Investing in something that requires a good weekend to establish and give you lifelong returns. There are many investments that state high yields and some are credible and some are not. This book is not here to give you the perfect mutual fund that will return 25% year after year. I am also not a professional financial consultant that has a hidden agenda for you to buy a Fund that they manage or receive a 1% management fee for suggesting that investment. The objective of this book is to teach you how to use regularly over the counter investments to achieve your financial goals and create financial independence. You can choose from many different investment types to achieve the 10%

Return on Investment (ROI) year after year after year. Anything more than 10% is a bonus and I suggest you use that Bonus to reduce the time it takes to achieve your financial goals than spending it on a new car.

So why am I talking about Passive Income, why is the term "passive income" so popular in society right now? Well, the reason is everyone wants the easy noncomplicated quick and dirty route. And the term passive income hits that itch on the head. Well investing as stated in this book shows the easy noncomplicated route that only needs a limited amount and knowledge to set up, and allows you to hit your financial goals. But it is not quick, it uses the power of time to build your wealth.

Level Out the Peaks and Valleys

In reference to the problem chapter. The problem with switching careers every 3.2 years, you need to: pick up and redo your budgets, redo your retirement planning, and redo your monthly expenses. The best place to be when you are interviewing is in a position of confidence and not desperation. To position yourself in the best position in these interviews be financially secure. It allows you to wait for the correct jobs, it allows you to negotiate the correct salary. You come into the situation in a place of power more than a place of need.

To span that gap between jobs and level out the peaks and valleys you need to know how much money you need on hand to survive. You need to make a budget for when you are between jobs and another budget for when you have a job. You need to have a 6-month account but that 6-month account needs to be a passive growing account as well. I personally have a 12 (you stated before that you have a 6 account) month/emergency account. I make sure that any of my active income savings goes into that account first before any other passive income account. I also make sure that the account has ½ of it invested in mutual funds returning ~10% a year and the other half into a saving bank account. So I can get my hand on it quickly if needed.

Let's say you need $3,000 a month to survive. And you average an unemployment gap between jobs of around 6 months. That means you need $18,000 a year to protect yourself from an unemployment gap. Having this saving account will let you span that unemployment gap with no need for a loan, no need for borrowing from family. Not having to borrow money will prevent you from getting over your head in bad debt or creating a burden. The issue with this though is that every 3 years you need to spend $18,000 to span the gap. That means you need to save $6,000 a year ($500 a month) just to protect you against these unemployment gaps. The purpose of this book is to show an alternative of waiting for the next time you need to fill a gap. Having a Passive Income Account paying your daily bills will allow you to use your active income to make your Passive Income Account bigger increasing your ability to take on more yearly expenses.

To prove this point I will take this example to the extreme. We will look at professions that have extremely large salaries with large unemployment gaps between jobs. There are many temp jobs but I will use Athletes and Artists as an example of these type of jobs. If you are an athlete, you will have times of negative salary, followed by huge salaries, followed by negative salaries. In the arts, you never know when you will land that TV series, having an album go to number 1, land that big part in the play. Many people can not handle these extremes and not knowing when the next paycheck is coming from. The saddest part of the story is that some athletes that play college ball never learned to balance a personal budget and are thrust into an extremely high salary. They surround himself/herself with people taking slices of the pie throughout the good years and run away during the bad years, leaving that person with physical body problems and now financial problems. Most Actors and Actresses have years of waiting tables before their big break which creates a more humble extreme temp worker. Still, most of them do not understand how to create a passive income account and live off that 1 big movie.

Example Number 1.

    Let's say that Jewel Smith is a singer-songwriter. She works as a waitress full time and sings each night in small dive bars. She sleeps on a friend's couch for years and lives off of $20,000 - $30,000 a year. With most of her savings going into new equipment, car repairs, and small business expenses, she does not have much to live on.

    At the age of 28, she releases her 4th album and one of the songs goes viral and climbs the charts. This lands her a US/Asia Tour opening for a huge star. After expenses, manager fees, lawyer fees, taxes, etc., she finds herself with $1 Million dollars in the bank. What does she do now, go buy John Lennon's Guitar? What does she want to do with the money? She doesn't want to return to the friend's couch but is humble enough to not crave a huge mansion either. This is where this system comes into play. The best advice is to find a good wealth manager to set up your passive income account and pay yourself 7% ($70,000) a year for the rest of Jewel's life. From there, live life and quit the waitress job and concentrate on what you do best. Take a small USO tour gig that creates more awareness than money. Allow the money to create opportunities that she did not have before. Live the life you always wanted to but did not have the ability to. For every album and tour past this point goes into the passive money account boosting the yearly salary higher and higher. So if Jewel's 8th Album+Tour gains her $500,000 that she puts into the Passive income account; that moves the total up to $1.5 million and a yearly salary of 7% = $105,000.. She does not get another hit after that and moves to a small mountain town playing once a week in a large bar where she is highly respected. And plays at charity events helping her community.

Honestly. If I was an artist this would be the dream. $70,000 a year and up is statistically proven to be, the level where people are comfortable and do not worry about money on a daily basis. They do not worry about the price of dinner, or if the world will end if the refrigerator conks out. So Jewel lives a happy life and makes all those years on the couch feel worth it.

Example Number 2

     Paul that was the Defenceman for the Seattle Sounders Soccer team for 6 years and played for the USA soccer team twice until he blows out his knee at the age of 28. Because he was a key player but not an all-star player, he walks away from the sport with $1 million in the bank. He moves out of the expensive city of Seattle and lives in his hometown collecting his 7% a year and enjoys life. He finds coaching and refereeing jobs from time to time. And he does not like to travel and he keeps his expenses low throughout the year. That financial security is enough to allow him to pick when and where he actively works.

Example Number 3

70% of all lottery winners lose all of the money within a couple of years and have a high level of bankruptcy. The same goes for people who get a large inheritance. Why? Well, the answer is simple, people that buy lottery tickets are typically people who are not good with money. So when they gain large amounts of money and they are still not good with money, they burn through it without even thinking about it. There is one lottery winner which was commissioning marble sculptures of the Blues Brothers characters. He was not good with money and was burning through it until it was all gone. But what if they put all of that $10 Million in a passive income account and took out only 7% each year. That means $700,000 a year or $2,000 a day to be spent. That is not enough for custom Marble statues but it is enough to take the family to Disney as a VIP each year. It is enough to buy the lake house you always had your eye on. But you need enough in the future to pay for the gas bill for that new house and the water bill for the pool you put in. Using the Passive income account allows you to budget your money to make sure you will never run out and go bankrupt.

Variable Income Converted into Steady Passive Income

What is a variable income and how can you convert it into a passive income account. A variable income means that your income changes year after year and is unpredictable across the years of employment. To explain this more, I will use Susan and Carly as examples. Susan is 21 and just became a professional athlete, she plays basketball for the WNBA and she is the star of her team. She signed a contract for 5 years at $750,000 to be paid yearly at $150,000 and has all her food/phone/rent and insurances paid for completely while employed. So she is single and has low expenses and high income, but she knows that this will only last as long as her knees do and she wants to prep for the time she does not have this job. Currently, while she is employed, she has a constant income, but she has no plan for what she will do after the WNBA. So she is identified as having a variable income.

Susan has a total of $24,000 in expenses each year for the time she is employed with this team. Her salary minus taxes and expenses leave her $88,500 each year to invest. So Susan invests this wisely and creates a Passive Income investment account and let it compound at 12% on average and let it accumulate to $560,000 in those 5 years. After that she can let it grow 10% after tax each year and pay herself a salary of $56k each year, year after year for the rest of her life. Pretty nice life if you can get it.

Carly is 45 and recently divorced. Carly lives in California and the couples financial value was split 50/50. After the sale of the house, the cash settlement was split and Carly received a check for $400,000 and has a 401k worth $400,000. She is currently unemployed but has been working on and off for the past 20 years with odd jobs as an interior designer and party planner and cook. Her yearly salary varied from $25,000 to $55,000 a year. Knowing that she can not afford to stay and live in California she moves to her home state of Kansas and gets a job as a baker at a local small town bakery for $25,000 a year. She loves the job but knows that the bakery might close due to the economy of the town. So Carly needs a long term plan to protect her from going without. She invested her $400,000 check and it is making on average 11% each year. She wants the account to grow over time so she reinvests 3% each year (good idea at age of 45). This means that she is paying herself ~6% after taxes. So that means that she pays herself $24,000 each year. Her normal expenses are around $35,000 each year trying to rebuild everything in Kansas. So that means she uses her active income to pay the difference and also reinvests the difference into the Passive Income account. After five years at the bakery, it decides to close on Carly's 50th birthday. She had to scramble to find a new job and did not find one for 2 years. She lowered her expenses to match her Passive Income account pull for those unemployment years. She found a job that paid her $45k a year in Indiana and purchased a new car increasing her expenses that year as well. She keeps investing all extra money into the Passive Income account. At the age of 55, Carly retires and lives off her Passive Income account 100%. At the age of 60, she starts pulling from her 401k as well. Even though she had an on and off again job with a variable wage she was able to keep the money flowing in from her Passive Income account, not only to pay her bills when she was not employed but to store enough money to retire early. This sounds amazing to me. Having that safety blanket and not scrabbling for the next available job, she was able to land jobs that she enjoyed and were flexible for her lifestyle. Having the pressure off her shoulders of "needing" a job allowed her to live her life the way she wanted to.

A couple of key points of this example. 1) She reduced her yearly expenses by moving to a cheaper location, 2) she invested all of her divorce money and did not spend it on a new house or new car. 3) She kept 3% invested to combat inflation each year. 4) She reinvested the "extra" money each year into the Passive Income account.

Total in Passive Income account.

Yearly Talley	Salary	Expenses
Year 1 - $400,000	$25,000	$35k = $24k+$11k
Year 2 - $426k = $400k + 12k (3%) +14K(reinvest)	$25,700	$36k = $26k+$10k
Year 3 - $455k = $426k + 13k (3%) +16K(reinvest)	$26,500	$37k = $27k+$10k
Year 4 - $485k = $455k + 13k (3%) +17K(reinvest)	$27,200	$38k = $29k+$9k
Year 5 - $517k = $485k + 14k (3%) +18K(reinvest)	$0	$31k = $31k
Year 6 - $532k = $517k + 15k (3%) +0K(reinvest)	$0	$32k = $32k
Year 7 - $548k = $532k + 16k (3%) +0K(reinvest)	$45,000	$41k = $33k+$8k
Year 8 - $601k = $548k + 16k (3%) +37K(reinvest)	$45,000	$42k = $36k+$6K
Year 9 - $658k = $601k + 18k (3%) +39K(reinvest)	$46,300	$43k = $39k+$4K
Year 10 -$720k = $658k + 20k (3%) +42K(reinvest)	$47,700	$45k = $43k+$2K

At the age of 55, Carly's account started paying 100% of her expenses. At the age of 60, she starts pulling from the 401K and uses that money to pay for better health and long term care insurances and uses what is left as a bonus to raise her standard of living.

The easiest way to make 1 Million Dollars

Everyone wants a million dollars. Who wouldn't? Weather that million is a symbol of retirement, a symbol for getting out of a dead end job, or a symbol of being able to pay off your parent's house; everyone wants 1 Million Dollars. It is a sign that you made it. This is why 90 Million Americans play the lottery each year. All trying to find a way out of their current situation and into the lap of luxury. If you are that person and you bought this book so you could achieve this goal, this is a sure fire way to become a Millionaire. This is the best way to creating a Million Dollars.

There a lot of getting rich quick "Passive Income" myths: (Selling on Amazon, Writing a Book, Real Estate with no money down) and various other get rich quick schemes selling the term "passive income". This is not that kind of Book. In this book we will teach you how to get rich the easy way, the only truly Passive income that exists. The others are active and also gobble up your money. These have been tried and found to be gambling with your money.

The path in this book is truly easy and truly passive. All you need to do is invest $3 dollars a day, or $90 each month. Store that $90 in a savings account and each year your investment will accumulate by $1,080. That is all you need to do. Again all you need to do is invest $90 each month and you will become a millionaire. I can not state this enough; it is that easy. To prove it, I will show you the easy math that will turn your $90 into $1Million Dollars.

How do you convert $90 into $1 Million?
If you invest a $90 a month into an account starting at the age of 21, that returns 11% CAGR, you will be a millionaire at age 65 and a half. Look at the Math

y=(Amount in Account *1.11) +Money to be invested each year.

Age	Amount in Account	Money to be invested each year
21	0	$1,080
22	$1,080	$1,080
23	$2,279	$1,080
24	$3,609	$1,080
25	$5,087	$1,080
26	$6,726	$1,080
27	$8,546	$1,080
28	$10,566	$1,080
29	$12,808	$1,080
30	$15,297	$1,080
31	$18,060	$1,080
32	$21,126	$1,080
33	$24,530	$1,080
34	$28,309	$1,080
35	$32,503	$1,080
36	$37,158	$1,080
37	$42,325	$1,080
38	$48,061	$1,080
39	$54,428	$1,080
40	$61,495	$1,080
41	$69,339	$1,080
42	$78,046	$1,080
43	$87,711	$1,080
44	$98,440	$1,080
45	$110,348	$1,080
46	$123,566	$1,080
47	$138,239	$1,080
48	$154,525	$1,080

49	$172,603	$1,080
50	$192,669	$1,080
51	$214,943	$1,080
52	$239,666	$1,080
53	$267,110	$1,080
54	$297,572	$1,080
55	$331,384	$1,080
56	$368,917	$1,080
57	$410,578	$1,080
58	$456,821	$1,080
59	$508,151	$1,080
60	$565,128	$1,080
61	$628,372	$1,080
62	$698,573	$1,080
63	$776,496	$1,080
64	$862,991	$1,080
65	$959,000	$1,080
66	$1,065,570	$1,080
67	$1,183,862	$1,080
68	$1,315,167	$1,080
69	$1,460,916	$1,080
70	$1,622,696	$1,080

    The Math is simple, it is not a huge complicated equation. The only thing that prevents people from doing this is themselves. 1 in 5 people does not invest in the company's retirement program because of many reasons. Whether it is choice paralysis, mistrust of the company, or just a lack of trust in the Stock market, there are many reasons why people tell themselves that the stock market will not work for them. If you only invest in the S&P500 you will be looking at an average return of 9.8% over the past 90 years. This is a fantastic return. It varies all the time, there are bad years and there are good years, but it is consistently returning good returns on average. Most people see a bad year and get out of it and this is how you lose your shirt in the stock market. The way to invest is just put money into what you think is the best mutual fund and close your eyes. Do not think about it and do not watch it daily., Just sit back and monitor it once a year to make sure that your return average is doing well. Mutual Funds can do better than the S&P 500, but not all do. On average, only 30% of actively managed funds do better than the S&P 500. So if you are not stock savvy you can just buy the Vanguard 500 Mutual Fund and sit back and know that your money will increase at a rate of 9.8%. This would take you 4 hours to set up an account and 10 minutes each year to reinvest. That is a truly passive account.

If you increase from $90 a month to $200 you will reach your million dollar goal early at the age of 58 instead of 65. If you can afford $500 a month you will reach it at 50. And if you increase it all the way to $1,000 a month then you reach 1 million dollars at the low age of 44. People everywhere want to have 1 Million dollars in the bank and all you need to do is invest $90 a month. But if you can afford $1,000 a month you can reach that goal in as little as 23 years.

Per Wikipedia, the average median US household income in 2017 is equal to $61,000 a year. That means that more than half of the US population should easily find $90 a month to invest in their retirement. Whereas the median retirement account is only $5,000 for people between age 32-61.
https://www.cnbc.com/2017/04/07/how-much-the-average-family-has-saved-for-retirement-at-every-age.html
 that means they are relying on Pension accounts, which are going away faster and faster, as is Social Security. This is not a good plan. Let's break that down. Private Companies (Not Government run) are removing pension plans for new employees and existing employees and even bankrupting on the pension plans for current retirees. With the average time, you spend with a company is 3 years, this means that you most likely will not become vested in any employers Pension plan. This $90 a month investment plan will fix that problem.

But wait a minute Kevin, what if I am not 21 and I want to also become a millionaire. The quick answer is to just count backward. I made a little cheat sheet for you to plan out

Years to build your account	Amount needed per month
45	$90
40	$150
35	$270
30	$460
25	$500
23	$1,000
20	$1,300
15	$2,500
10	$5,000

If you are 40 and want to be a millionaire by the age of 65 then you just need to invest $500 a month. That is only $6,000 a year!

The foundation that you will build up from.

The foundation of financial freedom is the first financial independence.

Financial Independence is not having to rely on others to meet your monthly budget and not allowing your family to fall into debt that you can not build a ladder out of.

Financial dependence is a "debt spiral" that most people can not get out of. A debt spiral starts like this. Jimmy is living paycheck to paycheck with no extra money going to savings. In this example, Jimmy can be making $30,000 to $80,000 a year in this example. Living from paycheck to paycheck is a common practice for many low to high earning families. Jimmy's car needs new tires at a cost of $700 and this month's budget does not have enough to pay for those tires. So Jimmy goes to the credit card with a 15% APR. Jimmy tries to pay off the $700 with $50 dollars per month. After 16 payments Jimmy will have paid $74 dollars in interest. The next month Jimmy gets hurt and has an Emergency bill of $1000 which also goes on the credit card. This means that Jimmy is paying for 15% more on his purchases over his monthly budget. This builds up over time, because of other emergency financial needs. Over a couple of years Jimmy builds up a credit card debt of $8000 and this can lead to Jimmy not paying more than he is charging which delay the pay off point. A portion of his paycheck goes to paying off his interest on his debt which decreases his take-home salary. The only way to pay for emergencies from this point on is to run to the credit card. This is called the debt spiral, making it harder and harder to get out of it.

     Step 1 is to develop an "Emergency Fund" to dip into when you have emergencies. This allows you to get through the emergency financial events. This is only to be used for true emergencies. The definition of an emergency is unexpected health costs, appliance failures, or unexpected car expenses. Not having to dip into the credit card will save you money long term. This fund can also be used as living expenses between jobs. For everyone, this amount can vary., I personally use a 6-month salary amount stored away in a separate bank savings account, and only draw from it in the cases of emergencies.

You need a good foundation. You need 6 months of expenses in a Savings account or other good liquid investment that you can get access to if you need it. This is for emergencies like a washer and dryer breaking or if you or your spouse loses your job and you need to float between jobs for 6 months of time. Saving accounts nowadays do not offer any interest, but everything is cyclical and in the early 2000s I used to have a rolling CD ladder and was earning 5% on my money. Not great, but something.

Why is the 6 months account needed? While you are building your passive income and Passive Income accounts, you need to know that if an emergency occurs you will have the money to address the issue. A modern day tale of debt spirals happens when someone does not have enough money to survive an emergency. This is not just a security fear, but also a financial wrong decision.

So step 1 is to create your 6 months emergency fund and keep it funded. So how much do you need? What are your current monthly expenses? Let's just call it $5,000 for this example. Just multiply it by 6 and you have $30,000. That is not to assume that you can not reduce your expenses to $3,000, but to make an appropriate buffer, assume your current salary. I try to use my salary to pay for any popup emergencies, but sometimes things happen. Some examples are new transmission in my car, a New Washer and Dryer, a lighting strike that fired my AC machine, TV, and Garage Door opener to name some of those emergencies. Those cost more than $1,000, so I needed to tap into the emergency fund to pay off the emergency. Just pay back into the account as soon as possible to get the amount back up to the total amount. You can invest your 6-month account into an investment and have a higher return on investment than 5% a year but you need to make sure that you can sell that investment any month of the year to pull money out to pay for emergencies as they come up. I also suggest that you separate out that money in its own investment or account, so you do not lump it into other investments. Treat it as its owns special account.

Step 2 is to pay off all high-interest rate loans including credit card debt. Paying off the debt is a return of 15% year after year. Using Jimmy's $8000 as an example, he would save $1200 a year in just interest payments. This is simple math. Do not invest in a mutual fund returning 10% a year when you could use that money to pay off your debt at 15% compounded.

Step 1 and Step 2 need to be complete before moving forward in this book. These steps are needed to build your financial independence. These two steps will save you more money than any other tips in this book. So you need to make sure that you completed these first. If you are using the credit card as you fall back, you can complete Step 2 before Step 1 if you prefer.

My rule of thumb is to maintain no debt with a rate of more than 6.5% APR. If you have personal or business debt with an interest rate or more than 6.5% leave this book right now and go after it. Double pay your interest until it is completely gone and then and only then come back to this book. If you are having difficulty with completing Step 1 and 2, there are many books that dive deep into budgeting and getting out of debt. Some of my favorites are here in no particular order. You should be able to find these at your local library as well.

The Total Money Makeover
By: Dave Ramsey

Zero Debt: The Ultimate Guide To Financial Freedom By: Lynnette Khalfani-Cox

So if you have paid off your large Debt items and you have your 6 months account, you are ready to look at creating your Passive Income accounts.

There are other long term investments that you need to know about. If your employer offers a 401K plan, it is an easy way to store that money away and forget about it. Most employers really want to see their employees happy. (Honestly, a happy employee is a good employee). So many companies offer a 401k or some sort of retirement program. I recommend using that 401K plan for four big reasons, and two reasons not to use it.

1) Company match. Most companies will match a certain percentage. A common match will be if you invest 6 percent, then the company will match 3 percent. Take this money and run. This is absolutely free money. You are stupid if you do not take this money. So if your income is $60,000 yearly and you invest 6% or $3,600 then the company pays you $1,800 into that account. $1,800 alone invested well will reach 1 Million dollars in about 37 years. And when you combine your $3,600 and the $1,800 into your investment then you have $5,400 invested. This gets you to 1 Million dollars in 27 years. That means you will be a millionaire at the age of 47.
2) Tax Break. A 401k is a retirement tax shelter similar to a Traditional IRA. This means that you are not taxed on the money that you invest. If you make $60,000 then that 6% will not be taxed, and your taxable income is decreased by $3,600 and so you will only be taxed on $56,400. This could save you more than $1,000 in taxes each year.
   +++ I would suggest a mix of traditional IRA and Roth IRA for tax reduction, but we will talk about in a another book+++
3) Set it and forget it. If you set up the 401k investment to always pull from your paycheck, you will not feel the pain of having to invest, you will not even know it is happening. The best way to invest is by not knowing it is happening. Keeping yourself out of the investment equation always results in more investments.

4) Investment fees are sometimes reduced. Because your account is combined with all other employees the companies shop around to get a better deal for their employees. This discount varies greatly, but if you do your homework you might find that your investments inside the 401k have a discounted fee. Not always the case so do your research.

The negative of 401ks.
1) Investment choices are not always the best. Holders of the accounts will typically only offer a limited catalog of investments that you can buy into. So do some research and find the best investments for you within that catalog. I search for the S&P500 option.
2) You can not get that money until you are at the age of 65. You can get your hands on that money in an extreme case, but you will have to deal with major fees and tax issues, removing many of the advantages of having that 401k. I would never recommend taking money out early. So your money is essentially locked up until the age of 65.

The positives out way the negatives by a landslide. And do not forget the number 1 rule. If you do not get that extra 3% match "You are an Idiot".

This book is about retiring early and locking up all your money until the age of 65 will not get you there. So what you are going to do is to invest in the retirement account at a level that gets you your match and a level that will keep you happy in your old age. You will also create an investment account outside of your 401k that will pay your bills until you reach the magic age of 60.

Create a Passive Income Account and Turn $10,000 into an infinite source of $1,000

Creating a Passive income account is so easy we can also call it a "Passive Income Account" because it outputs money each and every month. If you have $10,000 and you invest it wisely, you can return 10% each year, year after year. This is super easy to do. You can buy an investment that matches the S&P 500 in an investment called an ETF or electronically traded fund. The S&P 500 returns 9.8% and to use a simpler number we will use 10%. The S&P 500 averaged a yearly return of 9.8 percent for the past 90 Years. In the years of 2013-2017, it ranged -0.7% to 29.60%. So the account invested in the S&P 500 is volatile. But what I have found is; the highest returning investments are normally above-average volatility. So if you can handle the volatility, you can return much higher returns. The answer is yes, you can find higher returns on investment items. But here is the kicker; actively traded funds show better on certain years but on average underperform the index. Articles range in what the winning percentage is, but I have seen between 71%-80% of actively traded funds underperform against the indexes.

With that being said, I will give you my personal top 5 that I hope will outperform the 9.8% benchmark.

Name	Stock	15 Yr Return Average (Data as of 2017*)
Fidelity Large Growth	FDGRX	13.60%
Fidelity Blue Chip	FBGRX	10.80%
Fidelity Select Medical	FSMEX	13.80%
Fidelity International	FISMX	13.71%
TRowe Small Growth	FDGRX	12.02%

Expense ratio average around 0.8%

Again I am not a financial advisor, nor am I an endorser of these funds, nor am I paid by any financial institute. I am not responsible if these funds underperform their normal average return. Do not take my suggestion as a guarantee they will stay constant in the future. With any investment, there is always a risk. You need to do your own research and pick the investments that work best for you.

I spent 8 hours looking for the best mutual funds from Fidelity, T Rowe Price, and Vanguard and this is what I found out using Google and Morningstar. I am sure there are better funds out there and I am sure there are cheaper expense ratios and I am sure we could argue about which one or all to use. But I put these in the book to prove a point that there are common everyday funds made by large financial institutes returning an average of 12% after expense ratio. You can find funds out there that return 12% on the average year after year after year. Do not assume that the investments listed above will keep returning that same amount in the future. When doing my research to find my favorite investment, I look for one key attribute. I look at the 15 or 20-year return on investment. Looking out 15 years takes away the hot "fund of the day" and a long history of good performance. Of course, some of the hot tech stocks show much higher 5 yr return. But I am not looking for something that volatile. So the 15yr return average is what I am looking at when choosing a wise investment.

    You need to do your own research and find the right fund for you. Do not be upset if these funds that I have listed do not keep up with their annualized return average as stated. You can find funds out there that return 11.8% on the average year after year after year.

    So if you have $10,000 to invest wisely and you return 11.8%, you will get $1,180 yearly from the account. With a long term investment tax of 15% on the profit that you made, you can expect $1003 per every $10,000 invested. (Taxes on profit of $1,180 = $177) This is a data point that we will use over and over again throughout the rest of the book. It is easiest to use a 10% profit, but know that each year this amount will vary greatly and some years will have a negative profit. Remember that some of the more profitable investments are the most volatile and some years will have a negative profit and some years you will gain over 30%.

This steady investment that returns 10% a year of profit is a passive income account. This is what we are going to call "Passive Income" account as well. After the work of picking the good investment or investments, you will receive an income of $1,000 each year for the rest of your life.

If Amanda is 23 and has a life expectancy of 79 yrs that means she now has a Passive Income account that will pay her $1,000 for the next 56 years. or a total of $56,000 and have a trust fund that she can will to her children and then continue to pay that same amount year after year, going on to infinity. To do the simple math that $10k created $56k in passive income leaving the original investment of $10k. Turning $10k turns into $66k like it was magic.

Well, what can you do with only $1,000 a year? Well, you can pay for Natural Gas Bill each month, or your cable bill or your water and trash bill. Or maybe you use that $1,000 to pay off your car taxes each year, either way, it will take a little bit of the yearly bill burden off your shoulders.

So that is how you turn your $10,000 into an endless stream of money. And if you can hoard away more than $10,000 into your Passive Income account lets say $60,000, now you are getting $6,000 in Passive Income or an endless amount of car payments at a rate of $500 a month for the rest of your life. Wouldn't it be nice to have $500 a month of free money being created out of nothing?

How to find a 10%CAGR fund

In this chapter, I will teach you how to find a financial object what will return 10% each year every year. Again I Am a Saving Coach and Mentor, not a Financial Planner. So I will not tell you to invest in Apple Stock with all of your life savings hoping that the stock keeps returning the same results as past years.

But I will give you the two-step process that is very simple to do. Step one will take you literally 10 minutes and Step two will take you 50 minutes and within the hour you will have the first investment that you can use.

Step 1) Google it "Best Mutual Funds returning 10%". Find impartial blogs and lists that are not promoting their own brands. Look for company names that you trust, like Fidelity, T Rowe Price. Companies that have years of past success.
You are looking for something around 12-15% on average returns from the past 15 years. The 15 years annualized return is the most important Number. Do not be tempted in the flavor of the day. Don't look at Tesla Stock average returns. Not because it is a bad stock, but because you are looking for a good 15-year average when Tesla stock went public in 2010. Double check any research with Morningstar.com to find the 15-year return; never trust the

numbers from a single source. Make a list of any of these that have good annualized returns and pull the 15-year average. Out of 20 that you find make your top 10. When narrowing down from 20 to 5, try to pick from different categories. The more diversified, the shallower the lows will be.

Step 2) Convert to CAGR (Compound Annual Growth Rate) from AAGR (Average Annual Growth Rate). What you found during your research so far has been AAGR, and you need to target CAGR to make sure that you are averaging a 10% payout each year. This will remove some of the investments that have step ups and downs causing your AAGR to show high but really not paying out what you need. Find the past 15 years worth of returns and put that into a spreadsheet (Excel, Google Sheets) and start with $1000 in your spreadsheet. Multiple the $1,000 by the return from that first year. Take that new amount and multiply it is the return of the second year. Repeat this action for a total of 15 years. It should look like this.

Year	Return	Starting with $1,000
2000	-71%	$290
2001	47%	$426
2002	-34%	$281
2003	49%	$419
2004	201%	$1,262

2005	123%	$2,817
2006	18%	$3,325
2007	133%	$7,762
2008	-57%	$3,345
2009	147%	$8,258
2010	53%	$12,640
2011	26%	$15,871
2012	31%	$20,855
2013	5%	$21,985
2014	38%	$30,278

Once this is complete, you will have a resulting growth of your fictitious $1,000 invested. Let's use $30,300 as the return from that initial $1,000.

(Growth Amount / Initial Investment) ^ (1/15)
($30,300/$1000)^ (1/15) = 1.2553
which means that you returned ~25.5% each year, year after year. The AAGR for that same stock is 47% over that same time.

You might find that some of the funds that you were favoring are not the best because this simple conversation will remove some of the investments that were just too volatile.

This is a guide to find a steady return that we are going to use in the next chapters to grow from and rely on, and not have to manage. If you describe yourself as investment savvy and you think you can beat the market and or these investments go right ahead., But even if you do beat these simple investments, you will be trading time for money and your likelihood of beating the market is around 5%. If you actively trade and achieve outperforming the S&P500, you will still be a trading time of research for that extra income. Is your time worth it?

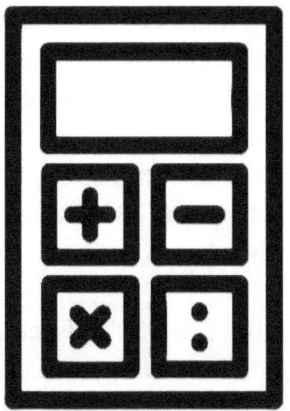

Inflation and harder Math

The simple math is easy and I will keep teaching this book using simple math. But the real world is full of more complex Math. I choose to ignore the more complex math for two factors.

1) I am trying to keep things simple for you the reader, in order to easily set your goals. It is much more important that you set a goal and go after it than worrying about more complex math that confuses everything and prevents someone from pursuing their financial goals. If you save $4 dollars a month and create retirement investments then you will most likely achieve your

financial goals. Anything more complex might keep readers away from investing and that is the last thing I would want to do. The only way to achieve your goals is to set an accurate goal and be consistent with your investing. Being a teacher over the past years, I find that the simpler I can make the material the more students will follow through with the teachings.

    2) It is truly not that important. Factors like Inflation and yearly raises from your job normally cancel out. The long term average inflation rate in the US is 3.22%. The average employment merit raises have less accurate estimates and many studies range between 2.7 and 4.6. The median of the top 5 studies on merit increase is 3.10%. This estimated merit raise does not account for transferring to a new job or being promoted in any way. When calculating your long term impact of those two items, it is a miniscule amount. If in 2020 your Electric bill averages $120 a month and you apply inflation each year at a rate of 3.22% than in 20 years (2040) your electric bill will be $226 a month. That might scare you but keep in mind that your active income will have increased at a similar rate.   If you were making $70,000 a year in 2020 than your annual salary will be $129,000 in the year 2040. The best way to truly compare those two rates is to look at the percentage of your salary that will go to your Electric Bill. So in the year 2020, the yearly electric bill is 2.06% of your salary. In the year of 2040, your electric bill will be 2.09% of your salary. That is only a difference of 0.03% of your salary. This is statically not significant. It is not worth your time to worry about

inflation for the period of time that you are employed and collecting an active income.

The only time that I will use inflation is for retirement calculations. If you retire in the year 2020 and you were predicting to only pay $120 for your electric bill for the next 20 years than you will not have enough money to pay for the electric bill in that year. If you stop investing in a Passive Income account and start using that account, then you need to worry about inflation as well. But I have done the research and calculations for you. I have turned the complex math into a simple multiplier that you can use to make sure that your account will last forever.

Based on your needs there are different levels of investment multipliers. If you are 45 years old and you plan to retire at the age of 65 and you only need your account to last 20 years when your 401k retirement accounts kick in then planning to have your account to last 20 years identifies the first level. At the 20 year level, the account will dwindle down each year, but it will last 20 years and at the 20th year the account will reach 0. The math is hard so I will give you a multiplier to be able to reach the full 20 years. Just multiply your goal amount by 1.05 which is an increase of 5%.

So if Noah is 45 and needs $6,000 a year to pay his house utilities, then Noah needs an account of $60,000 outputting 10% a year. Noah needs to multiply his goal of $60,000 by 1.05 and the result will be $63,000. This amount will last him 20 years pulling out $500 a month that first year and then increasing that output amount by 3% each year.

Yearly	Account	Yearly Pull
1	$63,000	$6,000
2	$63,300	$6,180
3	$63,450	$6,365
4	$63,430	$6,556
5	$63,216	$6,753
6	$62,785	$6,956
7	$62,108	$7,164
8	$61,154	$7,379
9	$59,890	$7,601
10	$58,279	$7,829
11	$56,278	$8,063
12	$53,842	$8,305
13	$50,921	$8,555
14	$47,458	$8,811
15	$43,393	$9,076
16	$38,657	$9,348
17	$33,175	$9,628
18	$26,864	$9,917
19	$19,633	$10,215
20	$11,382	$10,521

The next level is 30 year account. Again the account will decrease over time but it should last you 30 years but the account amount will equal 0 at the end of the 30 years. The 30 year multiplier is 1.23 or 23% increase.

The next level is the 50-year account. Again the account will decrease over time but it should last you 50 years but the account amount will equal 0 at the end of the 50 years. The 50-year multiplier is 1.375 or 37.5% increase. This is a great account for the end of life accounts. If you are 70 years old, you are not going to worry about your cable bill at the age of 120. This account will pay the bills for all 50 years of your life but will equal 0 at the end of it. No money will be left for your family after you leave. That depends on your state of mind. Do you want to work more years so our kids have a bigger trust fund or retire early and leave the family with no additional money? There are choices that you need to make.

The final level is what I call the 100-year level. At this level the account has enough that it does not decrease over time, it keeps increasing each year. This account is great if you are just starting out and you want to have the account forever, or you want to be a Rockefeller and hand your children an account that will last not only for them but also their grandkids. To achieve this level you need to apply a multiplier of 1.43 or increase your goal amount by 43%.

A quick guide for the Multipliers needed to conquer inflation issues.

Years until account is depleted	Multiplier
20 Year Account	1.05 Multiplier
30 Year Account	1.23 Multiplier
50 Year Account	1.375 Multiplier
100 Year Account *Account will not deplete*	1.43 Multiplier

The other way to look at it reduce the percentage of take out to reinvest a percentage back into the account: So instead of using 10% for your calculations you will use this new % instead of the 10%

Account	Percent of average Interest	New Percentage to use
20 Year Account	95.20%	9.5% if you are averaging 10%
30 Year Account	81.30%	8.13%
50 Year Account	72.70%	7.27%
100 Year Account	70.00%	7.00%

Imagine an account that pays for your mortgage, then wills to your children and it pay for their mortgage, and then wills to their children to pay for their mortgage. What a world that would be and you can create that account now.

I want to use a fun sci-fi example. The Cullen Family from the Twilight books. They are Rich, why are they rich, well they invested their active income accounts. Let's play a game if you turn into a Vampire tomorrow and you want to live life not worrying about money what do you do. You invest every dollar you get your hands on and you live off the interest. Your first couple of years will be hard, but with the growth of your account, it will get easier and easier. All active money goes to increasing your Passive Income Accounts and each year that account grows larger and larger, letting your money make more money. The Cullens are at a level where they do not need to work; they can make the choice to work, or study and grow their mind. With this book we will show you how to create 100-year accounts that will allow you to create that state of mind, allowing you to choose to work.

Relatable Characters

Throughout this book, I will use detailed calculations based on three levels of income and expenses. I will use three characters to demonstrate that it does not depend on your income to achieve your financial goals, it depends on how large your goals.

Let me introduce Peggy. Peggy and Mike are 23 years old. Peggy is a Personal Trainer making $36,000 a year. Mike is a carpenter and building his own business, but currently takes odd jobs and has a salary after investing in his own business of $23,000 a year. That is a total of $59,000. (This is the average US Household income in 2016) Peggy and Mike currently do not have children and rent an apartment in Georgia. They just got married and spent most of their nest egg on the wedding and honeymoon trip. Peggy and Mike do not know anything about money but Peggy works with clients that talk nothing but Stock trading, which has peaked her interest and wants to start investing but does not know where to start.

The income is $59,000
After Taxes Take Home = $47,000 (rounded for simplicity)
(Used https://smartasset.com/ to calculate estimated taxes)

That means a working budget of $3,900 per month

Peggy and Mike's Expenses are the following:
Apartment = $1,100 (Includes Water and Trash)
Utilities = $400
    Internet = $70
    Phones = $100
    Natural Gas = $100
    Electricity = $130
    Trash and water = $0 included in rent
Car Payment = $0
Gasoline for both cars = $400
Food and entertainment for 2 = $800
Insurances = $700

Average Monthly Expenses = $3,400

This means they have a surplus of $500 per month.

Their current Assets are the following:
Emergency Fund Bank Account $20,000
House equity: $0
401K Savings / IRAs: $0
Cars (2) Total = $30,000

Our next character is Thomas

Thomas is 40 years old and his engineering job pays him $90,000 a year. Thomas is Married to Sally and they have 2 children. Sally is a stay at home mom and receives $0 income and the kids are in every club and sports teams available. Cost of clubs, equipment and tutoring tally up to $500 a month. Thomas lives in Georgia and purchased a 4 bedroom house 10 years ago. Thomas is good at math but was not taught how to invest growing up. He was taught at an early age that saving is the key to making yourself financially secure, so he stores away as much as he can. He has been saving 10% out of his paycheck into his 401K since he started working with a company match of 3%.

His company has a Health insurance plan and he pays $500 a month for the Health plan which covers the family. He lives in his house that is worth $250,000 and has a loan interest of 3.5% and he invested 20% down payment so he does not pay any penalties or PMI, so the loan equals $200,000. They have paid into the house for the past 10 years leaving him with only $155,000 left on principle.

For Taxes, we will say that Thomas lives in GA with a tax rate of 4% and with an income of $81,000 he is in the 8.6% federal Tax bracket with a FICA of 7.65%. I used an online calculator. www.smartassesst.com and it was a useful website and showed an estimate of $16,700 in income taxes. But when you subtract 401K investments, healthcare expenses, Mortgage interest payments, itemized deductions, exemptions, 2 dependents, and other reductions, we will say that Thomas pays $12,000 each year for income taxes. Thomas pays 15% for long term capital gains on any investment that he has when that investment is sold outside of an IRA.

The income is $90,000
Invested into 401K (10%) = $9,000
After Taxes and 401K Take Home = $64,300 (rounded for simplicity)

That means a working budget of $5,300 per month

Thomas and family Expenses are the following:
House = $900
Utilities = $500
    Internet & Cable = $150
    Phones = $100
    Natural Gas = $80
    Electricity = $120
    Water =$50
Car Payment = $300
Gasoline for both cars = $400
Food and entertainment for 4 = $1600
Insurances = $600

Average Monthly = $4,300

This means they have a surplus of $1000 per month.

Their current Assets are the following:
Emergency Fund Bank Account $25,000
House equity: $100,000 (Current Value of $250k - the amount left on loan $155k)
401K Savings / IRAs: $325,000
Cars (2) Total = $50,000

The third friendly character is Steve
Steve is 60 years old and an Actor. Steve is married and has 3 children in college. Steve had a role in a large sitcom 10 years ago. He made a good living during that time and saved as much as he could. He stored up $900,000 in savings and is currently averaging $300,000 a year working on a new show. With all three kids in college, his is paying tuition expenses of $20,000 per child ($60,000 a year). The actors union created a 401K for Steve and invested a percentage of his earning throughout his career. Currently, the 401K has $1.6 Million in it and growing. Steve lives in California and purchased a 4 bedroom house 15 years ago and he paid off the mortgage 3 years ago to prep for the expense of college. The current house value is $1Million. Steve is very knowledgeable about investments and most of his savings are in the stock market already. He has been investing and keeps a   portfolio and averages around 9% per year.

The union has a health insurance plan and Steve pays $600 a month for the Health plan which covers the family. For Taxes, we will say that Steve lives in CA and claim 3 dependants and with a salary of $300,000 he is in the

25% federal Tax bracket, 9% state tax and a FICA of 4.79%. I used an online calculator. www.smartassesst.com and it was useful and showed an estimate of $116,000 in income taxes before removing 401K input and other expenses.

The income is $300,000
Invested into 401K (10%) = $30,000
After Taxes and 401K Take Home = $168,000 (rounded for simplicity)

That means a working budget of $14,000 per month

Steve and family Expenses are the following:
House = $0
Utilities = $800
    Internet & Cable = $200
    Phones = $200
    Natural Gas = $100
    Electricity = $200
    Water = $100
Car Payments = $1000
Gasoline for 4 cars = $800
Food and entertainment for 2 + 3 = $1600
College = $5,000
Insurance and house taxes = $1500

Average Monthly Expenses = $10,700

This means they have a surplus of $3300 per month.

Their current Assets are the following:
Emergency Fund Bank Account $80,000
Investments = 820,000
House equity: $1,000,000
401K Savings / IRAs: $1,600,000
Cars (4) Total = $160,000

Set Your Goal

I have shown you how making a Million is easy, especially if you have 45 years to build up a huge savings account. Everyone likes the idea of having a Million Dollars, but why. Do you really need $1 Million dollars to retire? The answer is NO!!!! It all depends on your current assets and current savings vs. what will be your retirement expenses. There are three consistent answers when people are asked the question; what will you do when you retire? The first is to relax and de-stress, the second is to spend more time with family and the third is to travel. Those are the typical answers given, and your particular order can change based on your priorities.

To explain how focusing on one of those three can change your retirement calculations. I will use an example of Jill and Dave which are 35 and have good solid jobs. They have a different kind of American Dream in Mind. They love to travel, and they want to retire early and travel around North America and then around Asia. They estimate that they will need $70,000 for traveling around North America for one year. They will be renting an RV and preparing their food in their RV to reduce costs. They currently have $70,000 in equity in the houses and cars to pay for that one year traveling in North America. After they sell their assets, they have that one year of travel covered, but they will not have any more equity to fall back on after that year is complete. So they will need to start all over again. After the trip around North America, Dave and Jill plan to relocate to the Philippines and teach English classes to build up their equity again. They have calculated that in the Philippines, they will need $1,200 a month for rent, food, and entertainment. They want to make sure they have a Passive Income account to pay for the years spent in the Philippines. They will need a yearly income of $14,400 a year to pay for expenses so they will need a Passive Income account with $144,000 in it. That is all this couple needs to retire. They plan to retire at the age of 40 and using the power of the US dollar to retire and relax in luxury. They plan to pick up small jobs in the Philippines like teaching to pay for inflation issues and insurances plus a separate nest egg to travel around Asia. But for the most part, retire at the age of 40 to the Philippines with only $144k in their pocket. This is 1/10th the amount that any financial advisor will tell you to invest to make a nice soft retirement. Currently, Dave and Jill have $20,000 in savings and make a combined income of $90,000 which allows them to save around $2,000 a month. This means they need to save for 5 years to store up an account of $144,000.

Imagine retiring and traveling the world at the age of 40. Accomplishing the task of traveling around the globe together and enjoying it while they are still young. This might seem like a non-traditional retirement, it might seem risky, and it might not be for everyone. I give this example to show an extreme that needs to be looked at in order to gauge your goals and objectives when planning how much you need to retire. It is all about what you have vs. what you need. The gap between those two points is what you need to fill with a Passive Income account + 401K and then you can retire. In the next several examples I will use the relatable characters to show you how to create accounts to keep the status quo. But remember Jill and Dave, to remind you that reducing retirement expenses can reduce the years it will take to retire early.

Pay your Cable Bill with Passive Income

So now that you know the basics of how the Passive Income account works, you can save enough money into the Passive Income account to pay for your yearly expenses. But all good things start small. So this chapter will start with a small goal. Create an account that will pay for your Cable Bill each and every month.

Setting a small goal is the best way to build momentum in creating an account that you can retire with. Let's find a way to pay for your Cable Bill for the rest of your life using a Passive income.
Let's say that on average you pay $100 a month for Cable/Internet. So how much do you need in a Passive Income account to output $100 a month to pay this Cable bill? The math is easy. If the bill comes each month and it is a steady $100 per month, you need to have $1,200 for the entire year to pay the bill each month. So if you need an output of $1,200 each year, you need to have an account that has $12,000 in it. So in simple terms if you have an account with $12,000 you will no longer need

your active income to pay for your Cable/Internet Bill. You are now financially independent from your cable bill.

If Peggy cuts her cable service and uses an Antenna for local news and she pays for Netflix each month, she lowers her monthly bill to $70 for internet, cable, and Netflix. Peggy needs only $840 a year, so Peggy only needs to save $8,400 for her Internet bill Passive Income Account.

So how long will it take for Peggy to build up her $8,400 account? If she invests all of her extra money in the account ($500 per month) it will take Peggy 1.5 years to accumulate the $8,400 needed for her Passive Income Cable Bill account.

Year 0 - 0
Year 1 - 6K
Year 2 - 6k + 6k + 708 (interest 11.8%) = 12.7k

There is a catch though. Inflation increases the cost of your utility on average by 3% each year. Peggy investigated her cable bills and yes it has been increasing over the past 5 years at a rate of 3% each year. The increase was sporadic over time, but after investigating Peggy's bills, it definitely went from $62 to $70 which is an increase of 3% each year.

Per www.fool.com the average cable bill went from $86 in 2010 to $123 in 2015 and predict $200 by 2020. That is more like 9.5% a year. Cable/internet bills are increasing faster than typical inflation. The reasons are many, but mostly because of additional cloud resources and new technologies; such as adding DVR boxes, adding HBO, adding Cloud storage, bundling, and others. But this is just a game that the cable company is playing against most of their clients. To prevent this, you just need to accept that the cable company is playing this game and you can use new technologies to control your cable bill. With newer technologies, there are other options than traditional cable. As of now, there are Netflix, Amazon, Hulu, HBO live and soon Disney will join the fight with Disney/ESPN online network. This allows your cable bill to be more ala cart, but having more options can lead to two different ways. You can buy all the options driving your cable cost up or you can get what you really need at a reduced amount. It is your choice.

Peggy and Mike do not need cable for their daily lives, so the internet and Netflix is good enough for them. But even at that level, inflation will take Peggy's cable/internet bill to $240 when she reaches the age of 65.

Assuming Peggy wants to plan ahead for this 3% increase on average each year, she needs to Grow her Passive Income account each year by 3%. So Peggy has two choices

1) Reach goal and invest 3% more each year. So using the calculation above Peggy reaches her goal of $8,400 in 1.5 years. But she needs to increase that account by 3% each year. 3% of

$8,400 is $252. So Peggy can invest $252 this year to grow her account to pay the increase for next year. The following year Peggy will need to invest $260 (an increase of 3% of the $252.
2) Option 2 is to reach a high goal that will be large enough that the inflation will not influence the output of her account.

So using Peggy and Mike as an example. They are aiming for $8,400 which will last them 20 years currently. They are 23 and want to aim for early retirement and travel the world. The thought initially that they would not need internet/cable when they are traveling, however, after research, they found that temporary internet in hostels and internet cafe can be relatively $80 a month in today's dollars. So they determined that they want to build a Passive Income Cable account to reach 100 years out. Their Internet/cable bill is $70 a month to $840 a year of expense.

So using the 100-year multiplier of 1.43 which means that the new goal amount is $12,012.
With the $500 extra dollars a month that Peggy and Mike are saving it will take a while to build up the account. So if they store that $6,000 a year and invest it every 4 months into a Passive Income account and build it up 10% on average each year

End of 4 months	$2,000,
After 8 Months	$4,066

After 1 Year $6,201
After 2 Years $13,043

      This means that Peggy will have a Passive Income account that they can use to pay their cable bill for the rest of their lives. This will remove the problem of worrying about how to pay internet bills while they are traveling along.

      For Thomas and Family, the example is a little different. First off Thomas is a sports fan and has the NFL package. This and other options raise his monthly bill to $150. This means the non-inflated goal is $18,000. Thomas and his wife are 40 years old and want to aim to retire at 65. They are investing in the 401k at a good rate. They are planning to retire on that 401k account at the age of 65. In the later chapter "How much do you need to retire" we will look in more detail of Thomas plan, but for now we will assume that at 65 years old Thomas will switch from using the Passive Income account and switch to using the 401k account. So Thomas is aiming for a 30-year account, which will take Thomas and family to the age of 70. That gives him 5 years overlap for good measure.

      So using the 30-year multiplier of 1.23 the new goal amount will be $22,140.
With the $1,000 extra dollars a month that Thomas and his family are saving it will take a bit of time to create an account large enough. If they store that $12,000 a year and invest it every 3 months the account and grow it on average 10% on average each year.

Year 0	$0
After 3 months	$3,000
After 6 Months	$6,075
After 9 months	$9,226
After 1 Year	$12,457
After 15 months	$15,768
After 18 Months	$19,163
After 21 months	$22,642
After 2 Years	$26,208

After 21 months Thomas will be 42 years old and will achieve the goal of having the $22k Passive Income account. Again this will last him until he is 70, this means an overlap of 3 years into his retirement accounts. At the age of 65, the account will still have $12,300 and the cable bill will average $3,770 a year / $314 a month. This will make the transition from a Passive Income account to living off the 401k much easier. Also planning a couple of years extra is a good practice since you never know which year will be a bad year for the stock market.

For Steve, things are a little different. Steve is 60 and wants to retire as soon as the current job depletes. Steve estimates that the current job should last another 5 years but knows that Hollywood decisions change quickly and each year his show could get canceled. So the plan is to start living from his $900,000 in savings and invest his salary as much as possible. He wants to pretend that the money from his current job is not needed and start living as if he is already retired, this way the transition is easy and allows him to test the budget that he is trying to live off of. Steve would like to set up separate Passive Income accounts for his utilities, taxes, and others. He is aiming for a 100-year account so he can pass it down to his next generation. So how much does Steve need to for the Cable Bill? Currently the cable bill $200, and costs $2,400 yearly. This requires an account worth $34,320 ($24,000 x 1.43). Steve starts this progression and sets aside some of the $900,000 in his savings for this utility account. Skip the next chapter if you want to see the math needed for Steve's full utility Passive Income account.

Never Worry About your Mortgage Payment Again

With the Cable bill example, it shows you that if you save, you can secure Need/want items with a Passive Money Account. That means you no longer need to think about paying that bill with active income. It is "free" for the rest of your life. But this simple account shows this can be done.

But honestly to make a large change in my life I personally need to set my heights high for me to follow through with it. Some people need to train for a marathon in order to get enough motivation to start running again. With a goal that large, people tend to be successful in following through. This can be the same for financial goals. Sometimes trying to reach small financial goals can be boring, so I gave myself this larger challenge to pay for my mortgage payment. I wanted to pay off my mortgage and get rid of all my "Debt". After some self evaluation, I knew that aiming for a Mortgage financial goal would be more successful than if I just aimed to pay off the cable bill. Now it is a personal choice as to what you aim for. I have read article after article looking for a secret path to pay off my mortgage early. I feel that your mortgage puts a weight on your shoulder that will endlessly never come off. More and more people are taking on a 30 year mortgage later in their lives pushing out their debt later and later. The need to get out from under that huge debt is even more important than ever. Being Mortgage free is what I started this whole Passive Income Account idea for me. I listened to Dave Ramsey for years in the early 2000s and almost all of the answers that he gave were Black and White answers, "Save more, Spend Less". But the one gray area that was the most intriguing, the most interesting, was the mortgage payments. There was a fan that called into his radio show and asked Dave this question "I have some extra money. Do I pay off my mortgage or invest that money"? I was driving in my car and I started answering the question for Dave thinking that I knew what Dave was going to say. I have been listening to Dave and I assumed that Dave would say "Invest that Money". At the time I was a single 22 year old with huge active income vs. expense situation and no mortgage or family expenses. I could invest in the stock market and get ~10 percent a year; I could invest in hundreds of other investments and still outperform a mortgage interest by 2x at the time. In mid 2003 the mortgage rates were ~5.5%. Apple stock which I owned at the time made 44% in 2003. The S&P 500 made

~28%. So it was a good year for investments. It was hard to imagine that anyone would not be in the stock market and make 2x, 3x, or even 8x the interest rate of the house. It was a no brainer in my head; of course you would not pay off your mortgage, you would invest that money and build up a nest egg that could pay off your mortgage later. But that is not what Dave said, and what he said shocked me. I pulled the car over, sat there, and thought about his quote that went something like this. "Well listener. The mortgage is the most emotional connected account that you have. Per the math, the choice is easy, but the mortgage account has an emotional connection to it. There is fear associated with not having a home. So ask yourself this? If your house was fully paid for, would you take out a loan against the house to invest in the stock market? If not, than you should pay off part of your loan." The point stuck with me. When it comes to some investments, there is more than just the math. More than black and white answers. More than a simple answer. I have thought about this gray area over and over again trying to find the correct way to tackle the mortgage equation. This book is the result of the research and calculations that I did 10 years ago. This chapter is the direct result of those calculations. I developed a different tactic for paying off your mortgage correctly, both with logic and with emotional security. At the risk of sounding like a Star Trek Vulcan, Emotions can be good and bad for your financial logic. The emotional choice of Dave's question will drive you to paying off the mortgage early, which is a great thing. It gives you a sense of pride that the house is your, it gives you a sense of freedom of not being in debt, it also lowers your monthly bills which is a great thing as well. The logical answer is to invest that money and make ~10% return on that money. If you do the math it will prove that it is the correct calculations. I will show my work and show how I first did the calculation before found the Passive Income Account method.

In my example, I will use Thomas and Family as an example.
To restate Thomas's example

Year left on his mortgage: 20
The Current mortgage balance is: $155,000
APR: 3.5%
Currently monthly payment: $900

Here is a simple Chart showing Thomas' loan payments.

Year	Left on Mortgage	Yearly Loan payment	Monthly Amount paid to Interest	Monthly Amount paid to Principal
0	$200,000.00	$10,777.08	$583.33	$314.76
1	$196,486.74	$10,777.08	$572.14	$325.95
2	$192,523.52	$10,777.08	$560.55	$337.54
3	$188,419.34	$10,777.08	$548.54	$349.55
4	$184,169.19	$10,777.08	$536.11	$361.98
5	$179,767.87	$10,777.08	$523.23	$374.86
6	$175,210.01	$10,777.08	$509.90	$388.19
7	$170,490.04	$10,777.08	$496.09	$402.00
8	$165,602.20	$10,777.08	$481.80	$416.29
9	$160,540.51	$10,777.08	$466.99	$431.10
10	$155,298.80	$10,777.08	$451.66	$446.43
11	$149,870.65	$10,777.08	$435.78	$462.31
12	$144,249.44	$10,777.08	$419.34	$478.75
13	$138,428.29	$10,777.08	$402.31	$495.78
14	$132,400.11	$10,777.08	$384.67	$513.42
15	$126,157.53	$10,777.08	$366.41	$531.68
16	$119,692.91	$10,777.08	$347.50	$550.59
17	$112,998.37	$10,777.08	$327.92	$570.17
18	$106,065.72	$10,777.08	$307.64	$590.45
19	$98,886.50	$10,777.08	$286.64	$611.45
20	$91,451.94	$10,777.08	$264.89	$633.20
21	$83,752.95	$10,777.08	$242.37	$655.72
22	$75,780.14	$10,777.08	$219.05	$679.04
23	$67,523.75	$10,777.08	$194.90	$703.19
24	$58,973.71	$10,777.08	$169.89	$728.20
25	$50,119.57	$10,777.08	$143.99	$754.10
26	$40,950.52	$10,777.08	$117.17	$780.92
27	$31,455.35	$10,777.08	$89.39	$808.70
28	$21,622.47	$10,777.08	$60.63	$837.46
29	$11,439.86	$10,777.08	$30.84	$867.25
End	($0.40)	$10,777.08	$0.00	$898.09

So currently Thomas has 20 more years left on his mortgage and is currently paying around the same amount of principal as interest.

Currently, Thomas has $1,000 a month of extra money to invest in a Passive Income Account. If Thomas invests all $1,000 into the account and that account averages 10% CAGR than that account will grow and be as large as the mortgage debt in 7.5 years (year 16.5 of the mortgage). At that time Thomas can pay off the mortgage with one big check. But before that point, the account can be large enough to start paying the mortgage payments each month allowing Thomas to stop using the active income to pay the mortgage and use the passive income account as the income to pay for the mortgage. This happens at 5.5 years (year 14.5 of the mortgage). In year 14.5 the Passive Income will make $685 a month in returns which is not enough to pay the full amount of the mortgage payment but the account is large enough that Thomas pulls all $900 each month and the account dwindles by $215 a month for the next several years and ends with $0 in the account.

So this means that after 5.5 years of investing $1000 a month Thomas can create an account that will pay off the mortgage completely over time. This is an amazing feat. If Thomas can wait until 6.5 years Thomas will have an account that will pay off the mortgage and then pay out $900 a year forever.

Year	Stored in Passive Income Account	Amount that can be pulled to pay off Mortgage	Decomposing Account	Left on Mortgage
10	$12,000	$100	($602,424)	$155,299
11	$25,200	$210	($398,397)	$149,871
12	$39,720	$331	($271,631)	$144,249
13	$55,692	$464	($156,389)	$138,428
14	$73,261	$611	($51,624)	$132,400
14.5	$82,200	$685	$227	$126,158
15	$92,587	$772	$43,617	$119,693
16	$113,846	$949	$130,200	$119,693
17	$137,231	$1,144	$208,912	$112,998

This is an interesting thought experiment that shows how using the extra cash can create an account large enough to pay off the mortgage. But remembering the Dave Ramsey Thought experiment. <u>What if Thomas inherits $155,000</u>, what paths would Thomas take to pay off the mortgage.

If Thomas Inherits $155k with 20 years left in the Mortgage

Path 1: <u>Pay off the mortgage Only.</u>
There is only one data point. Without the debt, he decides to use that $900 a month on luxuries. So Thomas financial windfall pays off his mortgage and has $0 in debt

and $0 in the bank. This means that no additional active income was spent on the Mortgage account.

Path 2: <u>Pay off the mortgage and use $900 (extra Money) to invest</u>. So in this path, Thomas writes a check for $155k to pay off the mortgage. Thomas will not have another monthly bill delivered to his house. Thomas takes the $900 a month that used to go to his mortgage payment and invested in a 10% CAGR account and compounded for 20 years, the account will result in an account worth $618,570.

Year	Account	Invest ec. Year
0	$0	$10,800
1	$10,800	$10,800
2	$22,680	$10,800
3	$35,748	$10,800
4	$50,123	$10,800
5	$65,935	$10,800
6	$83,329	$10,800
7	$102,461	$10,800
8	$123,508	$10,800
9	$146,658	$10,800
10	$172,124	$10,800
11	$200,137	$10,800
12	$230,950	$10,800
13	$264,845	$10,800
14	$302,130	$10,800
15	$343,143	$10,800
16	$388,257	$10,800
17	$437,883	$10,800
18	$492,471	$10,800
19	$552,518	$10,800
20	$618,570	$10,800

Path 3 <u>Invest and use returns to pay the mortgage payments (No other Active Income).</u>
In this path, Thomas will not pay off his mortgage with a check, but Thomas invests all $155k into a passive income account. That account will return 10% CAGR on average which is $15,500 a year. Thomas does not need the full $15k but he needs enough to pay for his mortgage payment. So he pulls out $10,800 a year from the account which is enough for him to pay his monthly bills. $10.8k is around 7% of the account which allows 3% to be reinvested each year growing the account at the same rate as inflation. This means that the account will grow at a rate or 3% for the next 20 years. This means the account will build to $280,000 at the end of 20 years. After the 20 years, Thomas will have the house paid off plus have an account that will pay out $900 for the rest of his life. An amazing situation.

Path 4: <u>Invest and still pay mortgage with Active Income.</u>
In this path, Thomas will act as if he did have a financial windfall and Invest all $155,000. He keeps using his active income to pay off his mortgage payments. He invests all of the $155k in an investment at a 10% CAGR account and compounded 100% of the money back into the account for 20 years the account will result in a net worth of $947,966. But we can not compare the $947 to the other paths since Thomas paid in $10,800 a year which totaled up to $216,000 over the 20 years. Thomas net tally is $731,966 ($947k - $216k).

Year	Account
0	$0
1	$155,000
2	$170,500
3	$187,550
4	$206,305
5	$226,936
6	$249,629
7	$274,592
8	$302,051
9	$332,256
10	$365,482
11	$402,030
12	$442,233
13	$486,456
14	$535,102
15	$588,612
16	$647,473
17	$712,221
18	$783,443
19	$861,787
20	$947,966

Comparing the 4 paths side by side.

	Saving Account Total	Extra Money to Spend	Amount of Salary going into Mortgage
Path 1	$0	$900 a Month	
Path 2	$618k	$0	
Path 3	$280k	$0	
Path 4	$732K	$0	$216k

Path 1 makes a great emotional choice, but without the mortgage payment Thomas finds it hard to keep discipline about his investing and spends his extra money on luxuries.

Path 2 makes a great choice if Thomas can be disciplined enough to keep investing his $900 each month. There are many apps and bank accounts that can be set to auto deposit money from one account into another. Done successfully you achieve the emotional gain of having the mortgage paid off and you are able to use that $900 to gain a large account of $618k, which can be used for retirement or other items. Just note that it took $216,000 of $900 investments to create this account

Path 3 is using the windfall to pay off his mortgage with no additional active income. This is the best scenario if Thomas does not want to put in any active income. This allows the money to return enough to pay off the mortgage plus leave a large account that can output much money each year.

Path 4 is the financial choice resulting in a great account that can be used to retire from or used for other reasons. The data shows the logical route is investing all of the $155k which results in an account ending in $732k. Again it took $216,000 to keep this path working.

Any of these is a useful path of Thomas's inheritance. All paths will be successful in relieving anxiety over paying the bills each month.

Pay your Monthly Bills with Passive Income

Following Thomas's example from the last chapter Thomas at the age of 45 now has his extra money growing at a rate of 3% a year. He also has his Passive Income Bills Account which means that he can reallocate the $900 to his extra cash.

    If Thomas wants to use his extra money to create a new Passive Income Account to pay for his monthly expenses. How much does Thomas need to save and how soon can he start using it. This chapter will look at jumping to the next level, trying to pay for all of the regular monthly bills. This will include the items for house utility bills, food (not entertainment), Gas for cars, and insurances.

    To take it slow I will take it to step by step. First Thomas will look at the utility bills. Thomas's monthly utility bills at age 40 totaled up to $500 a month including the cable/internet bill. So the simple math says Thomas needs $69,600 to have a Passive Income Account to pay for his other Bills. About half of what Thomas needed for the Mortgage account, which makes rational sense. The pattern of the utility bills being around half that of the mortgage is common for many people. Unlike the Mortgage account, the utility bill Passive Income account will not have an end date. So the Passive Income Utility account will need to adjust for inflation. Thomas is 45 and wants a Passive Income account of 100-year version, so he will use a multiplier of 1.43. So this means that Thomas needs an account of $99,500 for his utilities. At age 45 the amount of extra money has grown with his salary to $1,160 a month. With the $900 from money set aside for mortgage payments. So I will use $2,000 a month as Thomas's new investment amount. With $2k invested each month, it will take 4 years to complete.

This means that Thomas and his family no longer will need to worry about Mortgage payments or utilities. This means they will no longer need to worry about where they will live and no longer worry about the Gas being turned off. They can now just focus their efforts on paying for food and gas each month. Any job in the US can supply enough money for those expenses. This means that if Thomas wanted to quit his job and go work at a coffee shop as a barista for the rest of this life he could do that now. He could retire now and go teach English in a foreign country, there are so many opportunities available now.

If Thomas wanted to stay the status quo and keep all of his normal expenses then the next step after Utilities is Food, Insurance, and Gasoline for Cars. For Thomas, we will use a "need" (not want) of $2000 a month. This means a simple math account of $240,000, but that is in current dollars. To account for inflation and salary raises we need to raise the Monthly Bills up 3% per year and increase the Input of extra money also by 3% as well. This creates a little of a cat and mouse chase game. As Thomas's salary goes up throughout the years, his goal keeps getting larger. Thomas does not have to pay for Mortgage or Utilities anymore because the funding is coming from the Passive Income Account; this means he now has $2,400 of extra money (Today's Dollars). This with the salary growth of 3% means he has $3,200 at the age of 49 to invest in the next Passive Income Account. So at the age of 60 the need for the $240,000 now has become $529,400, which means it takes Thomas until the age of 57 to truly get to the amount that he needs to cover the expenses for Food, Insurance, and Gas for his cars. At this point, Thomas is so close to retirement.

Age	Amount in Passive Income Account	Input from Extra Money	Monthly Bills	Yearly Bills	Adjusted for Inflation
49	$0	$38,705	$2,688	$26,878	$382,479
50	$38,705	$39,866	$2,768	$27,685	$393,953
51	$82,441	$41,062	$2,852	$28,515	$405,772
52	$131,747	$42,294	$2,937	$29,371	$417,945
53	$187,216	$43,563	$3,025	$30,252	$430,483
54	$249,500	$44,869	$3,116	$31,159	$443,398
55	$319,319	$46,216	$3,209	$32,094	$456,699
56	$397,467	$47,602	$3,306	$33,057	$470,400
57	$484,816	$49,030	$3,405	$34,049	$484,512

This is amazing. Starting at the age of 40 Thomas now has an account that is large enough to pay for his Mortgage, Utilities, Food, Insurance and Gas for Cars. This is a financial independence that only people that work to invest and live from that investment will ever know. This is what separates the rich from the poor. For more of a holistic version of Thomas's calculations, skip to the "Enough to Retire" chapter for a slightly different approach. Thomas does not pull from his Passive Income Account while investing at the same time, making the calculation simpler but needs to be more discipline.

Never Pay a Car Payment Ever Again

First, look at the baseline of what people spend on cars each month on average. The average new vehicle loan hit a high of $31,099 (news article from CNBC on 3/2/18) https://www.cnbc.com/2018/03/01/americans-borrow-record-amounts-for-autos-even-as-interest-rates-rise.html. This equated to an average car payment of $515.00 a month

The average used car loan averaged $19,589 with an average monthly payment of $371.

So let's look at the average loss off that purchase. The Average Car over a 5 year period will be worth ~38% of the original value of the car. So the Average new car starting at $31,099 will be worth $11,817.62. Now there are a lot of factors. If you are buying a car that is not very common the value of the car can be as low as ~25% or as good as ~55%   Honda Pilots are some of the best when it comes to depreciation and average around ~50% of the original value after 5 years. (I have researched this and found various data on this ranging from 43.5% to 56% so we will use 50% for round numbers) Again this varies greatly based on many factors, so do your own research based on the car of your choice. So this means that the car value will be $15,549.50, or that you lost $15,549.50 for the ownership of the car over the 5 year time period. Or $3,110 per year average, or $259 per Month or $8.64 a day in depreciation alone.

So let's look at the total cost of the new vehicle If the purchase price of the vehicle is $31,099 and you need $3,000 as a down payment and tax and fees averaging of $2,672 (varies greatly based on state)? This will equate to a loan amount of $30,771 which equals a monthly payment of $553 based on an interest rate of 3%

and 5 year loan period. This means that you paid $2,404 in interest payments over the 5 years. For yearly insurance costs and yearly taxes, we will use $900 average per year for the 5 years. Or $75 per month.

So totaling this will mean that your monthly ownership cost of the car is $887 a month. So your investment of $40,675 turns into $15,549.50. Or a return of 38% of your money over 5 years. One of the worst investments that you can find. Now I know that you are screaming at this book and saying. "But I need a Car to get to work and everything else". Understood and I personally have a car for each adult in my household; just know that it is an expense, not an investment.

Now there are ways to reduce these expenses drastically.
1) <u>Reduce the Value of the car that you are purchasing:</u> If you have more expensive taste and that Land Rover is calling your name, just don't. We use this example to prove you can invest and fully invest your account.
2) <u>Buy a used version of the Vehicle:</u> If you buy the car that is 1 year old with 12,000 miles on it, you are looking at a reduction of $6,000 on average for that pilot or roughly 20% for the 1st year of depreciation. You still have the Manufacturer warranty, you still get that new car feel. If you can wait for the 2nd year you are looking at a 25% reduction. After that, the depreciation rate of change flattens out. Let's say that you want the Pilot, but you want it fully finished out with DVD

monitors and all other options. Well use this path to get the 2-year-old model but with all the options included.

3) <u>Keep the Vehicle longer than planned:</u> After the 5 years of your car loan is complete. You no longer have a car payment. If you invest that same amount of the car loan into Passive Income Account, you can start building up an account that you can use to pay your car payments. Currently, the average car ownership amount is 6 years. If you can push to 6 years, 7 years or even 8 years you will save so much more than buying new every 5 years.

Now that the baseline is set, let's talk about how to create a good investment around a large expense. So using a price of $31,099, let's look at a realistic monthly expense. If we had Honda Pilot before and we traded it in and the new loan amount is now ***$300.*** and you are planning to trade in 5 years from now. This means that you need to create Passive Income account that will be able to pay for the *$300*. So let's do the math on that.

We are going to use two examples. Kelly is 24 and still has her parent's old car worth $2,500. She is expecting a new kid and wants a bigger car. Her income is large enough that she can afford a new reliable Honda Pilot at the cost of $31,099. After Trade-in, fees, and taxes, she is at $30,000. She gets a loan for 3.1% which means a monthly car payment of $540. She plans to upgrade every 5 years with a new comparable Honda Pilot after the car payments are complete.

First year cost
Year 1) $3000 down payment + $540*12= $8830
Year 2) $540*12= $6480
Year 3) $540*12= $6480
Year 4) $540*12= $6480
Year 5) $540*12= $6480

Kelly want the new Honda Pilot and the price of a baseline Pilot has increased to $34,300, but her current Honda Pilot value is $15,550 which covers fees, taxes and down payment leaving her with a new loan amount of $20,000

Year 6) $360*12= $4320
Year 7) $360*12= $4320
Year 8) $360*12= $4320
Year 9) $360*12= $4320
Year 10) $360*12= $4320

 Kelly wants her 3rd new Honda Pilot and the price of a baseline Pilot has increased to $37,900, but her current Honda Pilot value is $17,150 which covers fees, taxes and down payment leaving her with a new loan amount of $20,800 with a monthly payment of $375

 But you can create an active income to pay for those expenses. Ignoring that initial down payment you need an account to pay your monthly payments. Let's say that you save during year 1-5 and create a passive income Car fund Account. So if Kelly saves $600 a month into a passive income account and it grows 10% a year, Kelly will create a passive income account with $43,900 in it producing a yearly check of $4390 to cover your car payments for the next several years. You will need to boost it with some of your active income to protect against inflation but you will never need to pay a car payment ever again. Imagine never having to pay for a car payment again, how much your life would be better if you did not have a car payment.

The hard math comes in when you look at inflation increasing the cost of cars over time. This means that her second Honda Pilot will cost more than the original amount. $31,100 * 1.02^5 = $34,336.

Now let's see if Kelly stretches the life of the car longer than 5 years. Well, let's do the Math.

First year cost
Year 1) $3000 down payment + $486*12= $8830
Year 2) $486*12= $5830
Year 3) $486*12= $5830
Year 4) $486*12= $5830
Year 5) $486*12= $5830
Year 6) $0
Year 7) $0
Year 8) $0

Kelly wants to upgrade to a 2-year-old Honda Pilot. The cost of the newer used car is now $24,850 ($35,000 new at 29% of depreciation) and her trade in value is now only $7,460, so after fees and taxes, the new loan is $17,500. Which is not a lot less than if she traded in at 5 years.

Year 9) $315*12= $3780
Year 10) $315*12= $3780
Year 11) $315*12= $3780
Year 12) $315*12= $3780
Year 13) $315*12= $3780
Year 14)
Year 15)
Year 16)

There are many benefits for this way of looking at the car payment amount and account needed.

Holding onto the car longer allows Kelly to put away all of the car payment into the car passive income account. For year 6,7,8 you can save $5830 a year which will equal $17,490.

1) Buying a slightly used car allows future car payment to be less
   With the lower car payment, you only need a passive account of $37,800 for those 5 years.
2) Holding onto the second car longer allows you to reduce how much you need to save up. Kelly can use these passive income payments to save up for more and buy a better 3rd car or she can use that gap to spread out the overall payments. So after some hard Math, if you have a Passive income account of $28,000 making 10% each year paying

the $3,780 each year dips the account down to $22,000 but in year 14,15,16 it builds back up to $29,000 which sets her up for the 3rd car.

So if the financial goal is a Passive income amount of $28,000 and you saved up $17,490 from years 6, 7, and 8. Kelly is left with a gap to save $10,510 or $72 a month for those first 8 years. So that means a good date night a month or cut the cable cord, could create an account so large that it pays for all of your car payments for the rest of your life.

Year 1) $3000 down payment + $486*12= $8830 Save $864
Year 2) $486*12= $5830 Save $864
Year 3) $486*12= $5830 Save $864
Year 4) $486*12= $5830 Save $864
Year 5) $486*12= $5830 Save $864
Year 6) $0   Save $6,694
Year 7) $0   Save $6,694
Year 8) $0   Save $6,694

The next Example is Steve:
Steve does well for himself and has a good income. He currently owns a 5-year-old Honda Pilot worth $15,000 and wants to trade in the Pilot for a New Land Rover. So let's talk about the details of this scenario.

The new Land Rover that Steve wants to buy costs $100,000 and has a bad depreciation rate of 60%. So, after 5 years of ownership of a Land Rover you are looking have a trade in value of $40,000. That means the cost of ownership is around $1,000 a month for just the depreciation alone. So let's do the numbers.

So Steve has his current vehicle worth $15,000. After Trade in, fees, and taxes he is at $86,000. He puts 10% down and a loan for 3.2% which means a monthly car payment of $1,400. He plans to upgrade every 5 years with a new Land Rover after the car payments are complete.

First year cost
Year 1) $1400*12= $16,800
Year 2) $1400*12= $16,800
Year 3) $1400*12= $16,800
Year 4) $1400*12= $16,800
Year 5) $1400*12= $16,800

Steve wants the new Land Rover and the price of a Land Rover has increased to $116,000, but his current Land Rover value is $40,000. After fees, taxes and down payment, he is left with a new loan amount of $76,000

Year 6) $1372*12= $16,464
Year 7) $1372*12= $16,464
Year 8) $1372*12= $16,464
Year 9) $1372*12= $16,464
Year 10) $1372*12= $16,464

This cycle repeats itself over and over again. To create an account to meet these needs, you need to create an account that pays out $17,000 a year. This means you need to find an account that is paying 10% and is a total of $170,000. So that means that having an account that is worth less than 2x the cost of the vehicle will result in an account that will pay for your car payments for the rest of your life. So if Steve creates that account then he has the ability to upgrade his Land Rover every 5 years and not worry about those car payments each year.

So given these Examples, you need to set your goal and your limit and do the simple math and find out how much you need to save in the Passive income account for you pay off your car payment each year. So saving $72 a month to $2,833 a month you can create an account that will create a passive income account to pay your car payments. An amazing way to save your money and create an account that allows you to live life simpler and with less stress.

How much do you need to retire?

Retiring is not something that only elderly people do. People are doing it all the time and at any age. It is just a math equation. It is all about monthly expenses vs. your interest payments. If you can live off $10,000 a year, then you can create an account of $100,000 and retire and live off of your interest payments.

What about living expenses? I have seen article after article of people retiring to Malaysia and spending less than $1,500 a month for total expenses including rent of a large 2,000 square foot apartment and cheap utilities and relatively great health care. I have seen many 20 something's live on the road in an RV and travel all around the world with a backpack and some good sneakers. I am not suggesting either of those as life to aim for, but I am using those as examples to prove a point that if you limit your monthly expenses, you do not need that magical 1 Million dollars needed to retire. So stop listening to your financial advisor that is selling your a 5 million dollar insurance policy at a cost of $170 a month.

Save that $170 a month invest it and create an account of $100,000 in 16.5 years and enjoy life.

So example 1)
Retire to Malaysia.
With an expense cost of ~$1,500 a month, you need $18,000 a year to live off of. So you need an account of $180,000 to retire at that level. You could sell your US house (Median value of US house is $188,000 in 2018) and with $0 extra dollars in saving you could fly yourself there and live off the interest. If you need to find yourself a great wealth manager that will send you monthly checks to you so you keep yourself on budget for the next several years.

The retired couple in the US, with no Mortgage payment and a car, fully paid off, could live on $2,000 a month. So if you just need $240,000 in a 10% account that will pay for your bills each year. This will not be an easy life and will need to live off the government for medical insurance, and you will need to work part-time to invest against inflation and also pay for a new car in 5 years.

But if you are on the track of the 1 million dollar retirement account, you can start evaluating what you are making in returns and when you can retire based on your expenses.

There is a big detail that you need to watch for though; the inflation. If you have 10 more years in your life, then inflation will not change your plans that much. But if you retire at 30, you need to watch the details of inflation and create an account that is large enough to not have to worry about inflation long term. *Refer to the inflation chapter for the calculations*

Retire Early

In the 90s 35% of the private employers were offering pensions to be competitive. This is no longer the case, and there is a growing level of antitrust of companies keeping their Pension fund fully vetted.
https://www.epi.org/blog/private-sector-pension-coverage-decline/
Relying on Social Security means that you are putting your fate in the hands of politicians of 20-40 years from now. That is great if you trust that American politicians will not touch your social security account over a 20 year time span. If you do not think that the politicians can influence your SS account, remember that in 1983 (while Ronald Reagan was president) Amendments were passed to increase the Full retirement age from 65 to 67 over a large period of time. So politicians have shown before then they can mess with your accounts.

But you want to retire early. Well, you can if you have a Passive Income Account that is fully funded. My personal plan is to build my Passive Income account large enough to get to age 60 and then live off of my 401k and any pension and or Social Security is a bonus. I am personally bullish on the 10% a year on the Passive Income account but I am ultra conservative on the SS and pension payouts. So those mix together to make a good mix. That way if I have a bad year from my investments I will have something to fall back on. This strategy also makes the math easier for examples. You need to find a mix that is correct for you.

Let's start with Peggy and Mike. Peggy and Mike are currently 23 with a household income of $59,000 a year. They have monthly expenses of $3,400 and save $500 a month. Or $40,800 a year in expenses and $6,000 a year into savings. Using simple math Peggy and Mike need 10x of their expenses ($408,000) in a Passive Income Account to live off the interest at their current status Quo. Peggy and Mike want to retire early and live off of the account for the rest of their lives. They want to retire around the age of 50 and are aiming for a 50-year account and die with pennies in their pocket. This means that Peggy and Mike need to use the multiplier of 1.375. So how long will it take for Peggy and Mike to store up the $561,000 that they need? Here is a chart to show Peggy and Mike's progression through the next several years.

Age	Yearly Expenses needed	Savings per year	Account amount	Possible Output
23	$40,800	$6,000	$0	$0
24	$40,800	$6,000	$6,000	$600
25	$40,800	$6,000	$12,600	$1,260
26	$40,800	$6,000	$19,860	$1,986
27	$40,800	$6,000	$27,846	$2,785
28	$40,800	$6,000	$36,631	$3,663
29	$40,800	$6,000	$46,294	$4,629
30	$40,800	$6,000	$56,923	$5,692
31	$40,800	$6,000	$68,615	$6,862
32	$40,800	$6,000	$81,477	$8,148
33	$40,800	$6,000	$95,625	$9,562
34	$40,800	$6,000	$111,187	$11,119
35	$40,800	$6,000	$128,306	$12,831
36	$40,800	$6,000	$147,136	$14,714
37	$40,800	$6,000	$167,850	$16,785
38	$40,800	$6,000	$190,635	$19,063
39	$40,800	$6,000	$215,698	$21,570
40	$40,800	$6,000	$243,268	$24,327
41	$40,800	$6,000	$273,595	$27,360
42	$40,800	$6,000	$306,955	$30,695

43	$40,800	$6,000	$343,650	$34,365
44	$40,800	$6,000	$384,015	$38,401
45	$40,800	$6,000	$428,416	$42,842
46	$40,800	$6,000	$477,258	$47,726
47	$40,800	$6,000	$530,984	$53,098
48	$40,800	$6,000	$590,082	$59,008
49	$40,800	$6,000	$655,091	$65,509
50	$40,800	$6,000	$726,600	$72,660

The chart shows that Mike and Peggy will hit their goal of having enough to pay bills with the interesting output at the age of 45 with a yearly interest payment of $42k with only yearly expenses of $41k. But to make sure they have the 50-year account they will hit that $561k goal at the age of 47.5. This also shows that if they keep going to the age of 50 they will be able to save a total of $726k outputting $72k, which means that they can increase their monthly expenses to $4.4k a month instead of their current $3.4k a month. The main trick is to not touch it. The compounding factor is what turns the $428k account into a $726k account. It is not the additional $6k a year that Peggy and Mike are investing. So not touching the account is the key to letting it grow. This means that the age of 45 Peggy and Mike have a choice in life. They can retire at the age of 45 and get part-time jobs as coffee baristas a couple of months a year or they can keep working and retire at the age of 47.5 and keep their current status quo or wait until the age of 50 and retire with $726,000.

Peggy and Mike are the average American family with the average household income, with no 401k or pension to fall back on, and viewing Social Security income as a bonus at the age of 60. This is amazing. With no external help, no employer help and no government help Mike and Peggy retire at an early age of 45 or 50. If they can do this then at least 50% of Americans can do the same.

To look at the complex math and add in inflation and salary raises into the equation it adds another 2 years of wait time to make up the difference between the complex math and the simple math. Again, this is not much of an actual difference.

Moving to Thomas and family Example.
Again Thomas is 40 with two kids and an income of $90k and a monthly expense of $4.3k and savings of $1k a month. Or $40,800 a year and $6,000 into savings a year. Using simple math Peggy and Mike need $408,000 in a Passive Income account to live off of, but Thomas has a large and well funded 401k account. And that is a big factor of defining the gap between his current age of 40 and the magic age of 60. First, we need to look at what is going to happen to his 401k account to know if Thomas can start living off his 401k at the age of 60. Thomas was diligent and stored 10% and his match of 3% for years and continues for every year of employment. Thomas has a current balance of $326k. If he finds an investment that

returns 10% within the list of possible investments in the 401k account than that $326k will turn into $3,000,000 dollars at the age of 60. That is 3 Million dollars that Thomas and his family can live off of. But Thomas does not want to wait until 60 to retire, he wants to retire earlier than that. What if Thomas stopped working now his 401k would grow without any more investment into it. If Thomas stopped investing into the 401k today that account would still reach $2,250,000. This is an amazing feat. At the age of 60 Thomas and Family expenses will reach $93,000 a year, But even with just the 2.225 Million dollars Thomas create a 100-year account and pull $155k a year to pay for his family's expenses. So Thomas's 401k is completely stacked and ready for his retirement, so any additional funding of this 401k is extra. After Thomas found out that his 401k was set for his retirement he started doing calculations to find out how soon he could retire.

So Thomas needs to span the gap between his current age of 40 and the age of 60 (when he can start pulling from his 401k). So how many years does Thomas need to work before he can retire early? Well, to keep the math simple we will guess which the possible years and then do the calculations to find out if it works. Here is a chart of Thomas saving his extra $12,000 a year.

Age	Yearly Expenses needed	Savings per year	Account amount
40	$51,600	$12,000	$0
41	$51,600	$12,000	$12,000
42	$51,600	$12,000	$25,200
43	$51,600	$12,000	$39,720
44	$51,600	$12,000	$55,692
45	$51,600	$12,000	$73,261
46	$51,600	$12,000	$92,587
47	$51,600	$12,000	$113,846
48	$51,600	$12,000	$137,231
49	$51,600	$12,000	$162,954
50	$51,600	$12,000	$191,249
51	$51,600	$12,000	$222,374
52	$51,600	$12,000	$256,611
53	$51,600	$12,000	$294,273
54	$51,600	$12,000	$335,700
55	$51,600	$12,000	$381,270
56	$51,600	$12,000	$431,397
57	$51,600	$12,000	$486,536
58	$51,600	$12,000	$547,190
59	$51,600	$12,000	$613,909
60	$51,600	$12,000	$687,300

This simple chart gives Thomas a road map that he can model multiple scenarios from. First is the conservative model. If Thomas works all the way to he is 60 years old the chart shows the account will grow as long as he is working and will reach $687k. So if Thomas works all the way to 60, he will have $3.6Million ($687 Passive + $3Mil 401K) to retire with.

But Thomas want to retire early, not and having $3.6 Mil when he retires, he wants to enjoy his retirement sooner than later with too much to spend. So what about 50 instead of 60? Will Thomas be able to retire at 50? Well, the Passive Income Account will reach $191k at the age of 50. If you divide that $191k by the 10 years between 50 and 60, you get $19k a year, and that is not enough to pay for his expenses each year. He will have to work longer than another 10 years.

So what about 55 instead of 60. Will Thomas be able to retire at 55? Well, the Passive Income Account will reach $381k at the age of 55. If you divide that $381k by the 5 years between 55 and 60, you get $76k a year, which is more than $51k needed for Thomas yearly expenses. Retiring at the age of 55 is something that Thomas never thought would be possible, but because he invested in the 401k and used his savings efficiently he is able to work past the age of 55 or start a different career. At the age of 60, he will have a 401K account that $2.8Mill at the age of 60. And can start drawing 7% each year until his fortune wills to his children. 7% a year will be around $200k a year and growing at 3% each year after year. So if Thomas can live "regularly" for the 5 years between 55 and 60, he can retire in the lap of luxury with $200k. And any pension and social security is a bonus on top of these calculations as well.

Thomas has one item that we have not figured in yet though. That is tuition for these two children to go to college. His oldest child entered when Thomas was 50 and the second entered when he was 54, which means 8 years of tuition payments between the ages of 50 and 58. Thomas converts his early retirement Passive Income Account into a Tuition Fund Passive Income Account for his children. This makes him just as happy about being about to pay for his kid's education as it would to retire early. Ultimately Thomas retires at the age of 60 with $3 Million in his 401k. This means that he can pull $210,000 a year which doubles his current status quo in future dollars. With the kids out of the house, fully retired, and extra money in their pockets Thomas and Sally decided to start a new chapter and moved to Italy and traveled around Europe during their retirement. This is a life that Thomas always wanted after spending a 1-week vacation in a remote part of Italy. What an amazing feat to pay for his kid's education and retire and move to Italy with his wife. Hard to ask for anything more than that.

The next example is Steve. Steve is 60 already, but Steve waited for enough tables when he was young to never walk away from a really good paying job. So Steve wants to stay working as long as Hollywood will let him. But can Steve retire now? At the age of 59 and ½, Steve can already pull from his 401k will no penalty. Steve has $1.6 Million in 401K and $820k in savings. Combined

Steve now has $2.4Million available. Steve wants his money to be handed down generation to generation in a trust fund. He also wants to call it the "Steve trust fund" and pay for college for his grandkids. So Steve wants his accounts to be 100-year accounts. If he averages 10 percent a year he can pull $169,000 a year. Why $169,000 a year. $169k is 7% of the total account. This is a trick that can be used no matter how much the account is worth. If you are making 10% in the investments than only take out 7% this leaves 3% in the account to increase the account by 3% each year to compensate for inflation. So Steve uses 7% and pays for his expenses. His current Expenses are $128k a year. This is an extra $40,000 a year. What an amazing thing. Not only can Steve live his nice life in California, but he can also do it with more ease than ever before and pass to his grandkids an account worth $2.4 Million to pay for their college education. It is nice to know that any dollar from the current job just raises the bar even higher each year.

You are finished!!!

So I showed you how to grow an investment account large enough to pay off your cable bill each month, Showed you have to have a Passive Income account to pay for your Mortgage payments, showed you how to budget a car payment, and how to retire early. The math is not hard, but the discipline to stay on track with your saving is more difficult than you will think. But at the end of the day, it is all about trading off that new car for an account to pay your bills for the next 50 years. It is ultimately your choice to which path to follow from this point forward. There is no better time to start than today. Book some time on your schedule this weekend and go online and select an online broker to start investing with and you will be started down the path to success. I hope that you find this information and calculations interesting and inspiring to drive you to your goals. With this information and this road map, you have the tools to retire early in your life and decide what to do next. Go After It!

www.ingramcontent.com/pod-product-compliance
Lightning Source LLC
Chambersburg PA
CBHW021824170526
45157CB00007B/2684